Pathway to Math 4

Student's Book

Glue your picture here.

Name

Richmond

Richmond

58 St Aldates
Oxford
OX1 1ST
United Kingdom

Pathway to Math Student's Book Level 4

First Edition: 2016
Eighth Reprint: January 2023
ISBN: 978-607-06-1258-9

Pathway to Math 4 is a collaborative work, created and designed by the Department of Educational Research of Santillana. Richmond adapted the project and created an English version.

Publisher: Justine Piekarowicz
Editorial Team: Matthew Bifano, Natalia Herrera, Duncan Jones, Jacaranda Ruiz
Pre-Press Coordinator: Daniel Santillán
Cover Design: Lourdes Arroyo

Cover Photograph: ©THINKSTOCK: iStock (mik38)

Illustrations: Martín Oyarce Gallardo, Paula Gutiérrez Fischman

Photographs: Archivo Santillana
©THINKSTOCK: Stockbyte pp. 153 (Jupiterimages).

Printed in Brazil by Forma Certa

Lote: 774584

Cod: 292712589

Introduction

Hi friends!

We are **Spot**  and **Kiki**  and we are here to welcome you to **Pathway to Math**. Follow us on the Pathway to Math, where learning becomes special. Do you want to know why?

- This pathway is full of magic, and everyone is welcome on it. You will find information, texts, pictures and activities presented in a simple and friendly manner. Here you will discover that learning is fun!
- This is a pathway where we can all learn to share and live together. The activities will help us reflect on our values and learn to respect others.
- This is a pathway open to people from all over the world where you can learn interactively with the help of the latest technology.

- This is a pathway full of challenges that involve finding solutions, developing math skills and applying calculation strategies that you and your classmates will work on together.

We will be with you every step of the way!
All you need is curiosity and the desire to learn.

How is your textbook organized?

Pathway to Math 4 is organized into five units. Here is what you will find in each unit.

Initial Pages

- Number and title of the unit
- Learning objectives
- Initial evaluation

Sections Organized by Learning Objectives

- Connecting
  Observe, read and answer
- Learning
- Practicing
- Analyzing
- Quiz Yourself

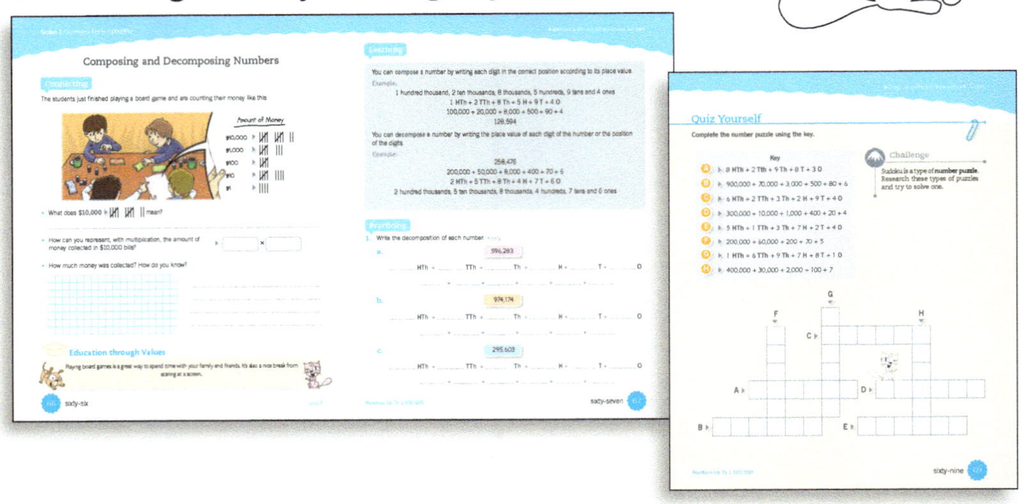

Fun Features

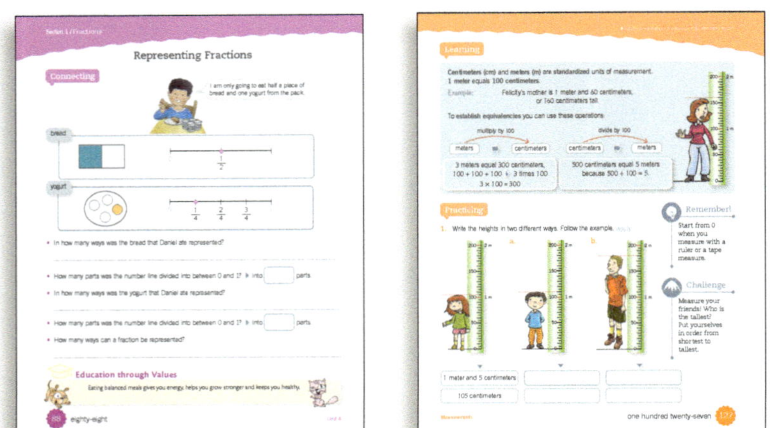

- Education through Values
- Did You Know...?
- Remember!
- Tip
- Word Focus
- Fun Fact!
- Challenge

Evaluation Pages

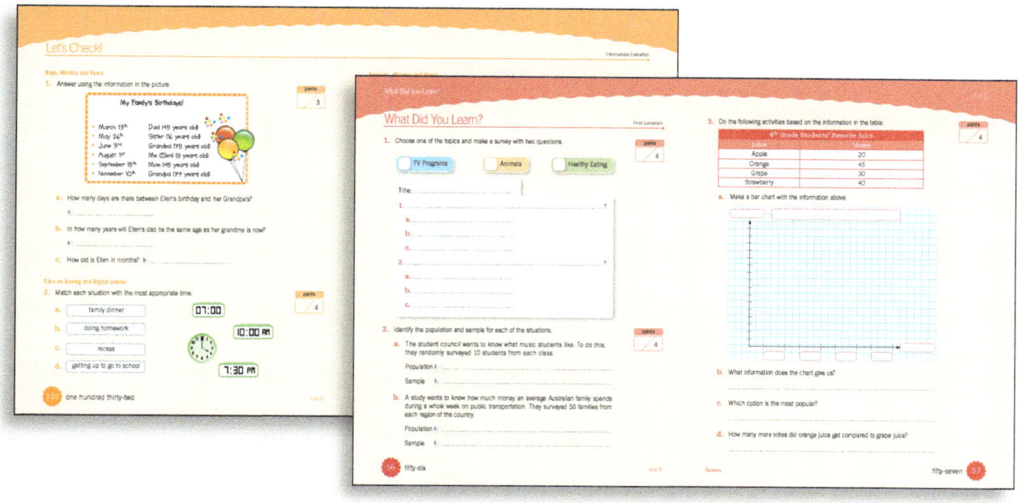

- What Do You Know?
  Initial Evaluation
- Let's Check!
  Intermediate Evaluation
- What Did You Learn?
  Final Evaluation

Special Pages

- Exam Strategies
- Test Study Pages
  Summary and Review

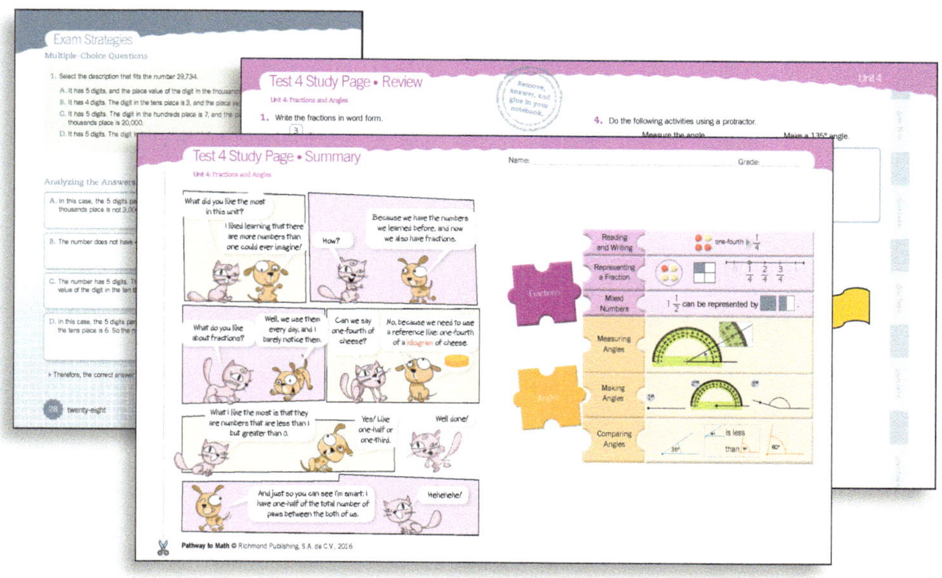

Support Pages

- Cutouts
- Activity Cards

Table of Contents

Unit 1

Numbers Up To 100,000

In this unit you will learn to:

- read, describe and represent numbers up to 100,000.
- count by 1,000s and 10,000s.
- represent numbers according to the place value of their digits.
- compose and decompose numbers.
- compare and put numbers up to 100,000 in order.
- have a positive attitude and trust your abilities.

Key Words

ten thousand

hundred thousand

number line

What Do You Know? Initial Evaluation

Look at the picture and answer.

1. How many miles must the car travel to reach Seattle?

   It must travel [ ] miles.

2. How many miles must the car travel to reach New York? Write your answer in words.

   It must travel ______________________

   ______________________ miles.

3. Which product has the **highest** price? Mark with a ✔.

   - [ ] bag of oranges
   - [ ] watermelon
   - [ ] bag of avocados

4. How much does it cost to buy one bag of oranges and one watermelon?

5. How much **more** expensive is one bag of oranges than one bag of avocados?

   expensive → cost a lot of money

Numbers Up To 100,000

Thousands, Ten Thousands and a Hundred Thousand

Connecting

John is looking at the following number cards.

- How many **digits** do the cards have?

10,000 has ☐ digits.   100,000 has ☐ digits.

- What digit is in the hundred thousands place in the number 100,000? How do you know?

The digit is ☐ because ______________________________

____

- How many 10,000 cards are needed to make the number on the orange card? Explain.

____

____

Learning

hundred thousand

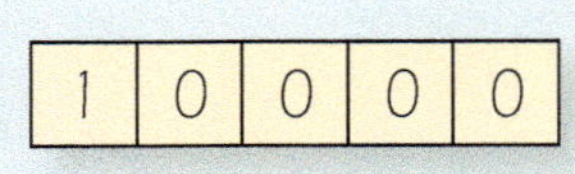

ten thousand

One **hundred thousand** is equal to
- ten ten thousands.
- one hundred thousands.

Practicing

1. Write the quantity of thousands, ten thousands and/or hundred thousands represented. Represent

a. 9 

stacks and 7 

stacks ▸

HT	TTh	Th

b. 9 

stacks and 3 

stacks ▸

HT	TTh	Th

c. 8 

stacks and 16 

stacks ▸

HT	TTh	Th

2. Complete the equivalencies with the correct number and answer. Apply

a.

HTh	TTh	Th	H	T	O
	6	0	0	0	0

equals ______________________ **O**.

HTh	TTh	Th	H	T	O
	4	0	0	0	0

equals ______________________ **H**.

HTh	TTh	Th	H	T	O
	7	8	0	0	0

equals ______________________ **Th**.

b. What process or strategy did you use to complete each equivalency?

____

____

Reading Numbers Up To 100,000

Connecting

Bert's teacher has written the following on the board:

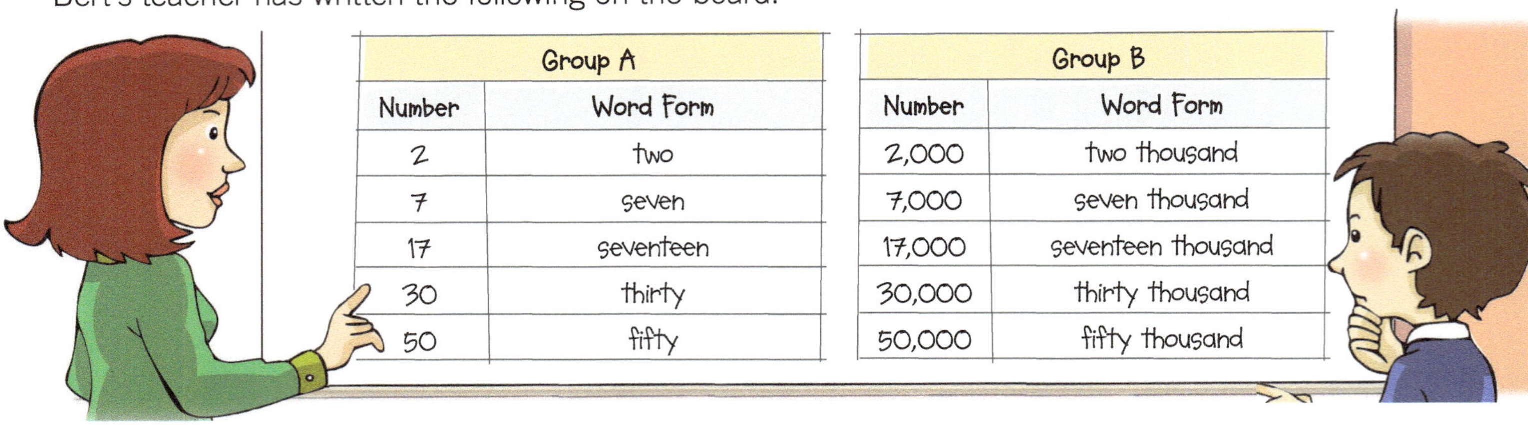

Group A	
Number	Word Form
2	two
7	seven
17	seventeen
30	thirty
50	fifty

Group B	
Number	Word Form
2,000	two thousand
7,000	seven thousand
17,000	seventeen thousand
30,000	thirty thousand
50,000	fifty thousand

- What similarities are there between the numbers in Group A and Group B?

  ____

  ____

- What difference do you see between the word form of the numbers in Group A and Group B?

  ____

  ____

- What similarities are there between the word form of the numbers in Group A and Group B?

  ____

  ____

- Is the following true? The number 27,027 is read as "two hundred seventy, twenty-seven."

  (Yes) (No), because ______________________________

  ____

- When you read the number 45,045 out loud, when do you say the word "thousand"? Why?

  ____

Learning

To **read numbers with five digits**, begin with the digit that is in the ten thousands place, followed by the thousands, hundreds, tens and finally, the ones.

The digits located in the thousands are read in the same way as a number with three digits but with the word **thousand** at the end. The comma separates the ones, tens and hundreds from the thousands family (thousands, ten thousands and hundred thousands).

Example:

58,258 is read:
fifty-eight thousand, two hundred fifty-eight

100,000 is read:
one hundred thousand

Remember!

Place a comma after the "thousand" and a hyphen (-) between the tens and ones digits.

Practicing

1. Match the numerical number with its word form. Relate

a. 78,780
b. 83,380
c. 38,380
d. 78,078
e. 38,000

- seventy-eight, seven hundred eighty
- seventy-eight thousand, seven hundred eighty
- thirty-eight, thirty-eight
- seventy-eight thousand, seventy-eight
- thirty-eight thousand, three hundred eighty
- thirty-eight thousand
- eighty-three thousand, three hundred eighty

2. Write in word form and answer. Represent

a. 34,052 ▶ ______________________________

b. 15,268 ▶ ______________________________

c. 71,309 ▶ ______________________________

- Which of the numbers was the easiest to write in word form? Why?

____

Counting Up To 100,000

Connecting

Schools in Chicago are taking part in a newspaper recycling campaign.

- How many newspapers are there in each pile? ▶ In each pile there are [ ] newspapers.
- What numbers did Robert count? ▶ ________ , ________ , ________
- Robert is counting by what? ▶ He is counting by [ ].
- Mark the place value of the digit that changed in the numbers Robert counted.

☐ ten thousands ☐ thousands ☐ hundred thousands

Learning

To count by 1,000s (thousands), change the number in the thousands place.

To count by 10,000s (ten thousands), change the number in the ten thousands place.

Counting **forward** by 1,000s:

25,259 , 26,259 , 27,259 , 28,259 , 29,259 , 30,259 , ...

Counting **backward** by 10,000s:

94,335 , 84,335 , 74,335 , 64,335 , 54,335 , 44,335 , ...

Learning

1. Complete the sequences by counting by 1,000s or 10,000s. Interpret

a. 0, 10,000, 20,000, 30,000, ____, …

b. 25,200, 24,200, 23,200, 22,200, ____, …

c. 35,540, 36,540, 37,540, 38,540, ____, …

d. 95,050, 85,050, 75,050, 65,050, ____, …

e. 12,006, 22,006, 32,006, 42,006, ____, …

2. Complete the sequences, counting by: Apply

Tip

Find the logical pattern to continue a number sequence.

a. 1,000s.

37,092, 38,092, ____, ____, ____, ____, …

62,450, 61,450, ____, ____, ____, ____, …

100,000, 99,000, ____, ____, ____, ____, …

b. 10,000s.

22,823, 32,823, ____, ____, ____, ____, …

74,609, 64,609, ____, ____, ____, ____, …

91,350, 81,350, ____, ____, ____, ____, …

Place Value

Connecting

- What is the **smallest** number that can be made with the digits? ▶ ______.
- What strategy did you use to make the number? Explain.

______

______

- Which digit is in each position? Complete.

HTh	TTh	Th	H	T	O

- What is the **largest** number that can be made with the same digits? ▶ ______.
- If you used the same digits, why is one **larger** and the other one **smaller**? Explain.

______

______

Education through Values

Recycling newspapers helps save trees. What other items can we recycle to help protect our planet?

Learning

The **value** of digits depends on their **position** in a number.

Example:
The five-digit numbers 28,000 and 82,000 are made with the same digits but represent different numbers, since the digits are in different positions.

28,000				
TTh	Th	H	T	O
2	8	0	0	0

82,000				
TTh	Th	H	T	O
8	2	0	0	0

2 in the number 28,000 has a **value** of 20,000 in the **ten thousands place**.
in the number 82,000 has a **value** of 2,000 in the **thousands place**.

8 in the number 28,000 has a **value** of 8,000 in the **thousands place**.
in the number 82,000 has a **value** of 80,000 in the **ten thousands place**.

Practicing

1. Circle the numbers that have a value of 8,000 in the thousands place. Interpret

18,092 93,728 38,991 81,590

80,007 83,857 58,104

2. Complete the table according to the highlighted digit. Apply

	Number	Position	Place Value
	29,167	thousands place	9,000
a.	86,903		
b.	48,257		
c.	93,430		
d.	76,345		
e.	67,221		

Composing and Decomposing Numbers

Connecting

Mike is counting the money he will deposit in the bank.

deposit: put money into the bank

Money	Quantity
10,000	7
1,000	2
100	8
10	9
1	5

- How much money will Mike deposit in all?

7 x 10,000 + 2 x 1,000 + ________ + ________ + ________

70,000 + ________ + ________ + ________ + ________

He will deposit [ ] dollars in all.

Tip

Composing and decomposing are inverse strategies.

Learning

Numbers can be analyzed by composing and decomposing them.

Composing: we write each digit in the correct position according to place value.

Example:

3 ten thousands	,	7 thousands	,	5 hundreds	,	4 tens	and	3 ones
3 **TTh**	+	7 **Th**	+	5 **H**	+	4 **T**	+	3 **O**
30,000	+	7,000	+	500	+	40	+	3

37,543

Decomposing: we write the place value of each digit of the number.

Example: 52,891

50,000	+	2,000	+	800	+	90	+	1
5 **TTh**	+	2 **Th**	+	8 **H**	+	9 **T**	+	1 **O**
5 ten thousands	,	2 thousands	,	8 hundreds	,	9 tens	and	1 one

Practicing

1. Match the numbers to their decomposition. Relate

a.	17,408	80,000 + 40 + 1
b.	75,916	7 **TTh** + 5 **Th** + 9 **H** + 1 **T** + 6 **O**
c.	80,041	10,000 + 7,000 + 400 + 8
d.	90,719	9 **TTh** + 7 **H** + 1 **T** + 9 **O**

2. Complete the composition or decomposition of the numbers. Apply

a. 82,730 = ____ **TTh** + ____ **Th** + ____ **H** + ____ **T** + ____ **O**

b. 18,302 = ____ **TTh** + ____ **Th** + ____ **H** + ____ **T** + ____ **O**

c. 63, 892 = ____ **TTh** + ____ **Th** + ____ **H** + ____ **T** + ____ **O**

d. ______ = 6 **TTh** + 2 **H** + 5 **T** + 1 **O**

e. ______ = 8 **TTh** + 9 **Th** + 4 **H** + 7 **T** + 3 **O**

f. ______ = 1 **TTh** + 3 **Th** + 0 **H** + 3 **T** + 9 **O**

Quiz Yourself

Find the following numbers in the crossword puzzle. They can be horizontal or vertical.

- three thousand, five hundred ninety-eight
- sixty-two thousand, fourteen
- two thousand, seven hundred sixty-one
- 7 **TTh** + 6 **Th** + 4 **H** + 5 **T** + 9 **O**
- 9 **Th** + 9 **H** + 3 **T** + 8 **O**
- 2 **TTh** + 3 **Th** + 8 **H** + 1 **T** + 6 **O**
- 6 **TTh** + 4 **Th** + 5 **H** + 9 **T** + 8 **O**

NUMBER SEARCH

6	9	2	6	5	7	4	9	0	1
4	1	5	8	7	6	2	0	1	4
5	9	7	3	2	3	7	7	2	9
9	0	3	5	2	7	6	4	5	9
8	6	4	9	7	1	1	0	5	3
4	2	3	8	1	6	7	3	5	8

Order and Comparison of Numbers

Comparing and Putting Numbers in Order Using a Place Value Chart

Connecting

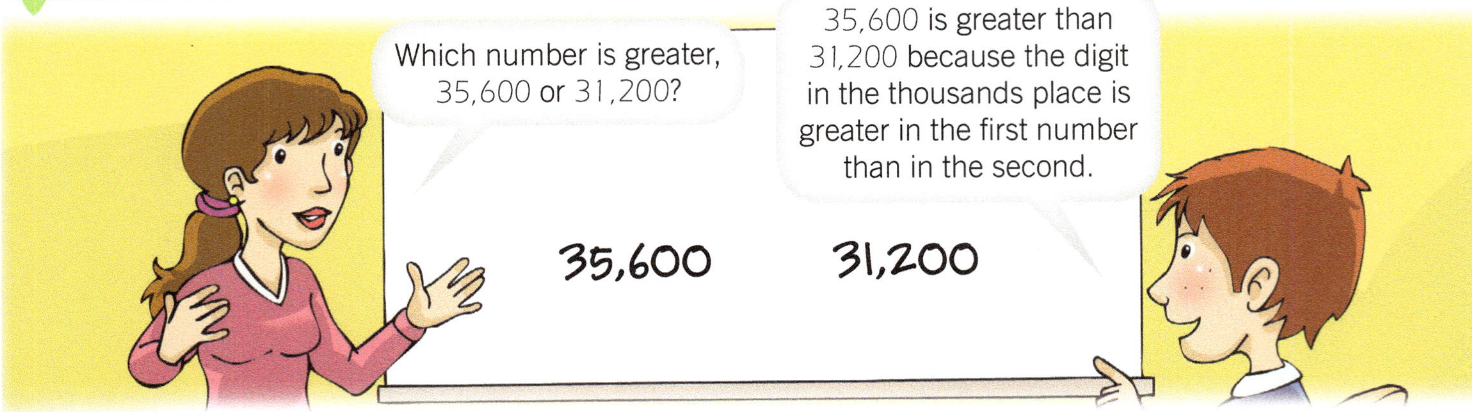

- Is Brian correct? Why or why not?

  Yes No , because ______________________________

  ____

- What process did you use to compare the numbers?

  ____

  ____

Remember!

If two numbers have a different number of digits, the one that has more digits is the greater number.

Learning

To **compare** numbers with **the same number of digits**, you can use a place value chart. Using this chart, values of digits can be compared, from left to right, digit by digit.

Example:

TTh	Th	H	T	O
3	7	0	0	0

TTh	Th	H	T	O
3	9	0	0	0

30,000 = 30,000

7,000 < 9,000

39,000 **is greater than** 37,000

37,000 **is less than** 39,000

Practicing

1. Circle the digits that allow you to compare the numbers. Then write which number is greater. Understand

a.

TTh	Th	H	T	O
8	5	2	3	5

TTh	Th	H	T	O
2	1	5	6	3

__________ is greater than __________.

b.

TTh	Th	H	T	O
6	3	4	5	3

TTh	Th	H	T	O
6	8	7	2	3

__________ is __________ than __________.

c.

TTh	Th	H	T	O
9	1	5	0	2

TTh	Th	H	T	O
9	1	5	0	0

__________ is __________ than __________.

2. Compare the following numbers using the place value chart and write >, < or =. Apply

a. 51,381 ◯ 51,928

TTh	Th	H	T	O

TTh	Th	H	T	O

b. 64,974 ◯ 64,923

TTh	Th	H	T	O

TTh	Th	H	T	O

c. 83,521 ◯ 84,521

TTh	Th	H	T	O

TTh	Th	H	T	O

Remember!

The symbols used to compare are:

> **greater than**
< **less than**
= **equal to**

Comparing and Putting Numbers in Order on a Number Line

Connecting

a space between two things

- What intervals is the number line divided into?

- Toward which side of the number line would the numbers 17,500 and 19,500 be located? Why?

- Toward which side of the number line are the numbers smaller? And greater? Explain.

- Between which numbers should the number 21,500 be placed by the student? Explain.

- Where would 23,500 and 24,500 be located on the number line? Explain.

Learning

To **compare and put numbers** in order, a **number line** can be used.
A number is **less than** another number if it is located more toward the left on a number line.
A number is **greater than** another number if it is located more toward the right on a number line.

Example:

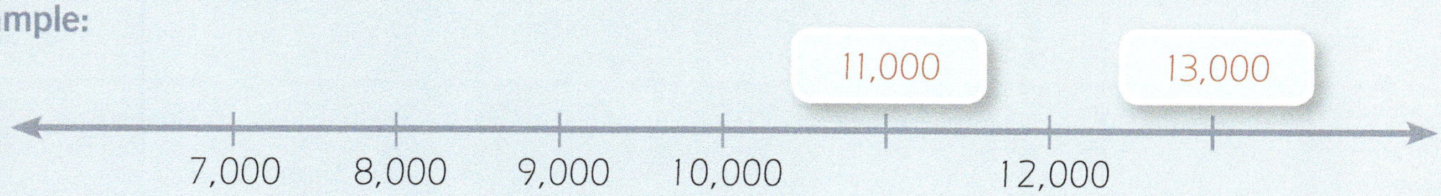

11,000 is to the left of 12,000 and is 1,000 less. ▸ 11,000 < 12,000

13,000 is to the right of 12,000 and is 1,000 greater. ▸ 13,000 > 12,000

Therefore, 11,000 < 13,000.

Practicing

1. Place the numbers on the number line. Then answer. Represent

a. 5,000 , 16,000 , 8,000 , 15,000 , 11,000 , 4,000

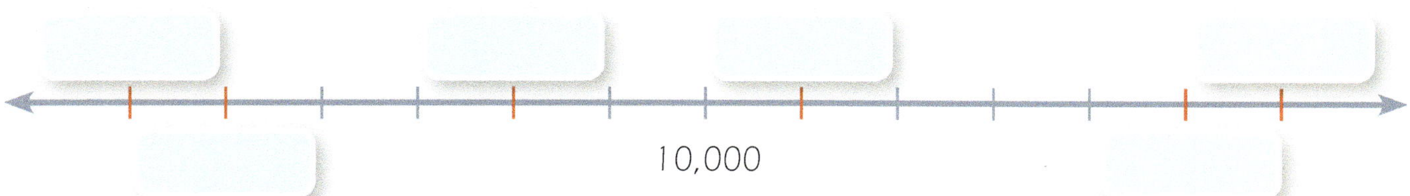

Which is the **greatest** number? ▸ ______

b. 35,600 , 34,900 , 35,700 , 35,000 , 35,500 , 35,100

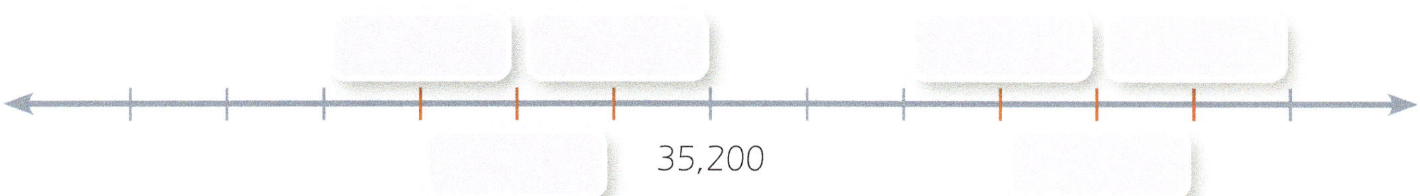

Which is the **smallest** number? ▸ ______

2. Mark the intervals on the number lines and place the numbers. Represent

a. 63,500 , 62,100 , 63,400 , 63,700 , 62,500 , 63,600

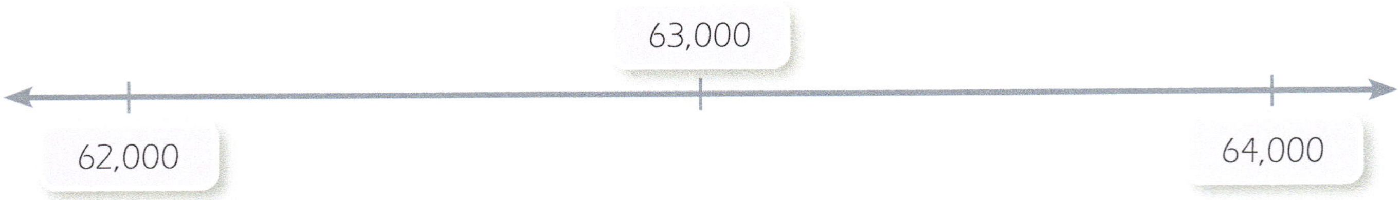

b. 37,000 , 42,000 , 44,000 , 39,000 , 41,000 , 36,000

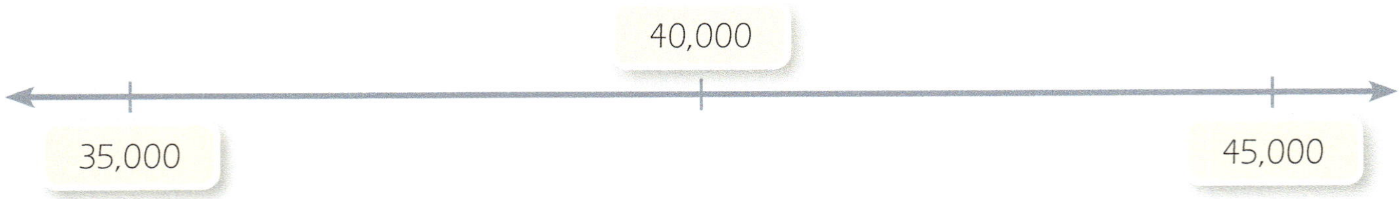

c. 42,000 , 55,000 , 59,000 , 49,000 , 45,000 , 51,000

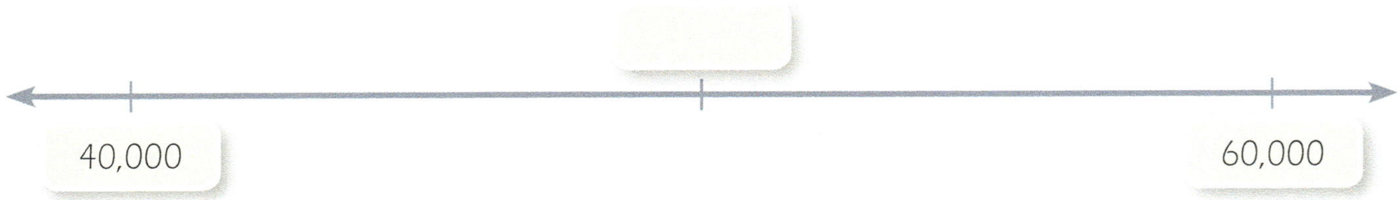

d. 81,120 , 81,230 , 81,190 , 81,240 , 81,150 , 81,280

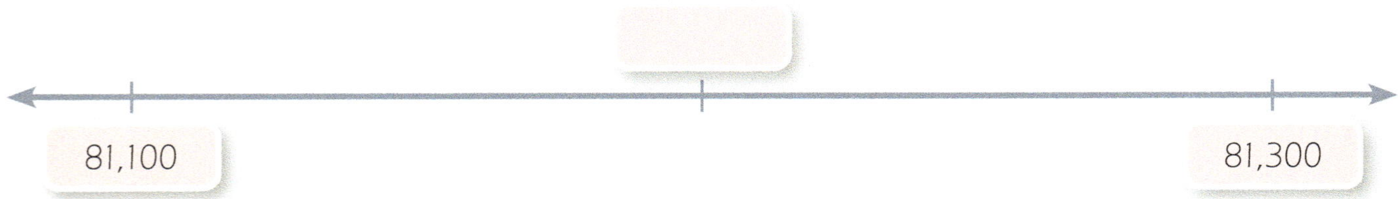

3. Look at the number line and answer. Analyze

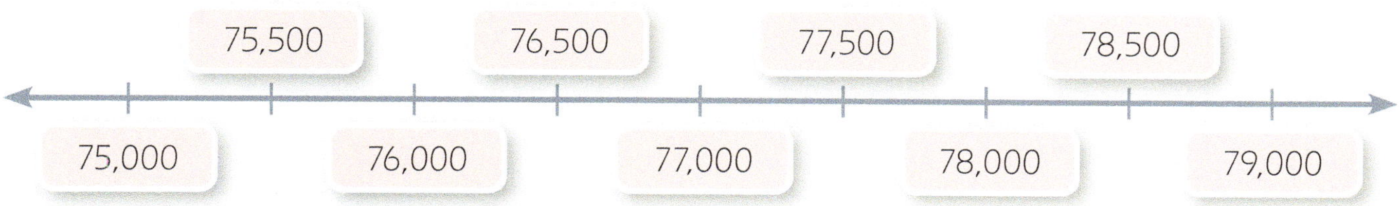

a. Which numbers on the number line are **less than** 76,500? Which are **greater**? Choose one for each.

[ ] < 76,500 < [ ]

b. What numbers could be placed between 77,000 and 77,500? Write three.

[ ] [ ] [ ]

Quiz Yourself

Complete.

- Using the place value chart, compare the following numbers.

25,680 , 25,670 , 25,590

TTh	Th	H	T	O

TTh	Th	H	T	O

TTh	Th	H	T	O

[ ] < [ ] < [ ]

- Place the previous numbers on the number line.

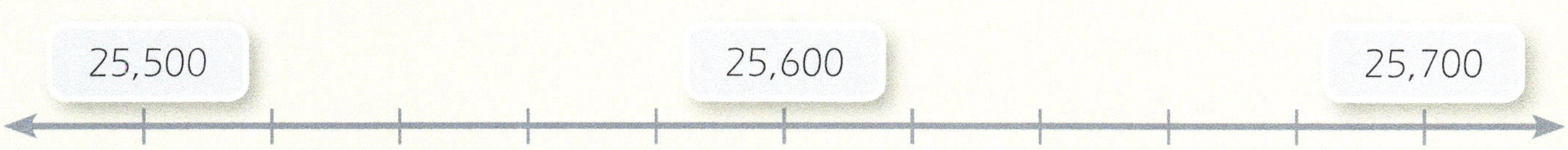

Let's Check!

Thousands, Ten Thousands and Hundred Thousands

1. Write the number of thousands, ten thousands and/or hundred thousands that are represented by the bills.

points
/2

HTh	TTh	Th

Reading Numbers Up To 100,000

2. Write the following numbers in word form.

points
/3

a. 78,351 ▶ ______________________________

____

b. 13,908 ▶ ______________________________

____

c. 60,742 ▶ ______________________________

____

Counting Up To 100,000

3. Continue the sequence, counting by:

points
/2

a. 1,000s.

58,301 , 59,301 , ____ , ____ , ____ , ...

b. 10,000s.

64,413 , ____ , 44,413 , ____ , ____ , ...

Place Value

4. Complete according to the highlighted digit.

points
/ 7

	Number	Position	Place Value
a.	38,924		
b.	13,872		
c.	92,563		
d.	56,280		
e.	21,450		
f.	70,382		
g.	48,600		

Composing and Decomposing Numbers

5. Write the composition or decomposition of the numbers.

points
/ 5

a. 70,000 + 3,000 + 200 + 90 + 5 = ______

b. 80,000 + 4,000 + 300 + 70 + 9 = ______

c. 23,985 = ______ + ______ + ______ + ______ + ______

d. 67,142 = ______ + ______ + ______ + ______ + ______

e. 44,753 = ______ + ______ + ______ + ______ + ______

Exam Strategies

Multiple-Choice Questions

1. Select the description that fits the number 29,734.

A. It has 5 digits, and the place value of the digit in the thousands place is 3,000.

B. It has 4 digits. The digit in the tens place is 3, and the place value of the hundreds digit is 500.

C. It has 5 digits. The digit in the hundreds place is 7, and the place value of the digit in the ten thousands place is 20,000.

D. It has 5 digits. The digit in the ones place is double the amount of the digit in the tens place.

Analyzing the Answers

A. In this case, the 5 digits part is correct, but the place value of the digit in the thousands place is not 3,000.

29,734

B. The number does not have 4 digits. It has 5, so this can't be the answer.

29,734

C. The number has 5 digits. The digit in the hundreds place is 7, and the place value of the digit in the ten thousands place is 20,000.

D. In this case, the 5 digits part is correct, but double the amount of the digit in the tens place is 6. So the number described has a 6 in the ones place.

29,734

▸ Therefore, the correct answer is **C**.

1. A B C D

What Did You Learn?

Final Evaluation

1. Write the numbers or the word form.

points
/ 6

a. ninety-two thousand, three hundred eighty-two ▶ [ ]

b. twenty thousand, five hundred four ▶ [ ]

c. fifty-eight thousand, four hundred thirteen ▶ [ ]

d. 32,901 ▶ ______________________

e. 29,018 ▶ ______________________

f. 87,470 ▶ ______________________

2. Follow each direction to answer.

points
/ 2

a. Count forward by 1,000s.

What is the fifth number if the first number is 27,903? ▶ [ ]

b. Count backward by 10,000s from 92,825.

What is the third number? ▶ [ ]

3. Use composition or decomposition to complete.

points
/ 4

Number	Decomposition	
25,300		
	60,000 + 40 + 3	
		8 **TTh** + 5 **Th** + 4 **H** + 9 **O**
	2,000 + 800 + 60 + 9	

points
/3

4. Put the following numbers in order on the number line. Then write them as indicated.

a. 63,890 , 63,590 , 63,390 , 63,790 , 63,490 , 63,690

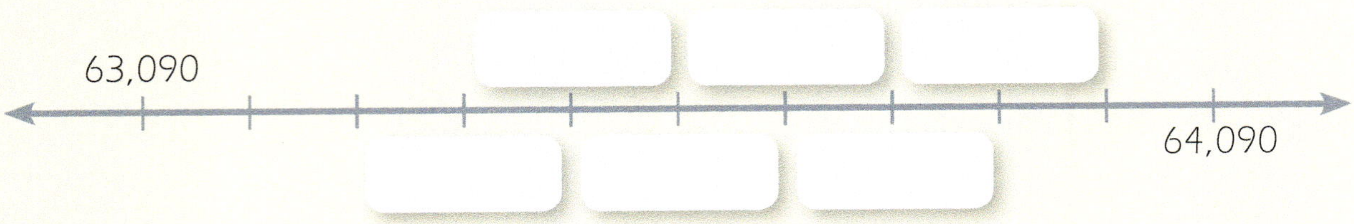

From least to greatest:

________ , ________ , ________ , ________ , ________ , ________

b. 89,500 , 85,500 , 87,500 , 88,500 , 84,500 , 86,500

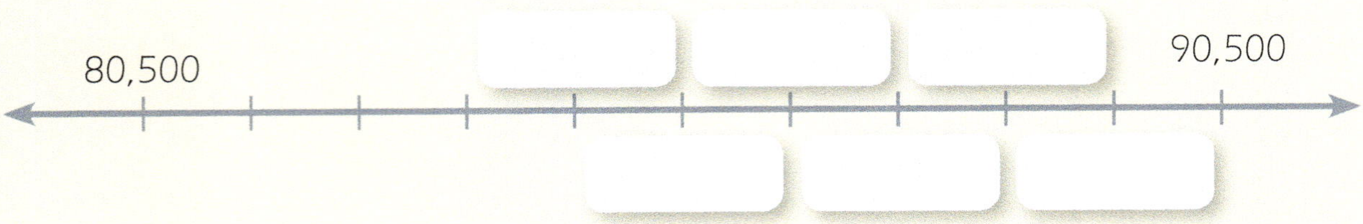

From greatest to least:

________ , ________ , ________ , ________ , ________ , ________

c. 69,800 , 70,100 , 69,400 , 69,700 , 70,200 , 69,600

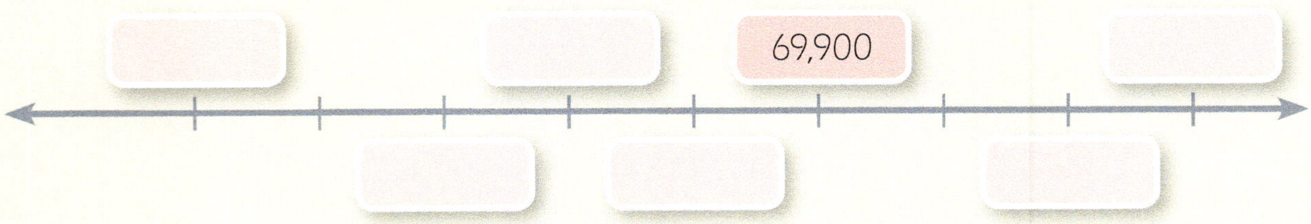

From greatest to least:

________ , ________ , ________ , ________ , ________ , ________

Mark the correct answer with an ✗.

5. Using the signs below, which city has fifty-four thousand, one hundred seventy-four people?

points
/ 3

A. Apple Valley

B. Livermore

C. Gilroy

D. Claremont

6. How is forty thousand, three hundred sixty written using numbers?

A. 40,306

B. 40,360

C. 41,360

D. 43,600

7. Which number continues the sequence?

37,250 , 38,250 , 39,250 , ______ , ...

A. 39,300

B. 40,200

C. 40,250

D. 41,250

points
/ 4

8. What value does the digit 7 have in the number 73,591?

A. 70

B. 700

C. 7,000

D. 70,000

9. Which is the decomposition of 47,809 according to its place value?

A. 4 **T** + 7 **O** + 8 **H** + 9 **O**

B. 4 **Th** + 7 **H** + 8 **T** + 9 **O**

C. 4 **TTh** + 7 **Th** + 8 **H** + 9 **O**

D. 4 **TTh** + 7 **Th** + 8 **H** + 9 **T**

10. Which of the following comparisons is **correct**?

A. 76,592 > 67,943

B. 59,118 < 51,504

C. 83,406 < 83,298

D. 16,894 > 19,341

11. Which is the correct decomposition of 80,304?

A. 8 thousands, 3 hundreds and 4 ones

B. 8 **TTh** + 3 **H** + 4 **T**

C. 8 **TTh** + 3 **Th** + 9 **H** + 4 **T**

D. 80,000 + 300 + 4

points

/ 4

12. How do you read the number 5,094?

A. Five thousand, ninety-four

B. Five hundred, ninety-four

C. Five thousand, nine hundred four

D. Five thousand, nine hundred forty

13. How do you write twenty-four thousand, two hundred four?

A. 24,204

B. 24,024

C. 24,240

D. 20,424

14. In which number is the digit in the ten thousands place 6?

A. 34,760

B. 54,632

C. 61,204

D. 86,751

15. What is the place value of the digit 8 in the number 45,082?

A. 80

B. 800

C. 8,000

D. 80,000

Find Test 1 Study Page

Unit 2 Surveys

Key Words

survey

population

sample

In this unit you will learn to:

- understand a survey and its objectives.
- analyze and compare the data from a survey.
- read and interpret pictographs and simple bar charts with a scale.
- show interest and curiosity in learning math.

What Do You Know? Initial Evaluation

Look at the picture and answer.

1. Look at the results of the first round. Complete the chart and answer.

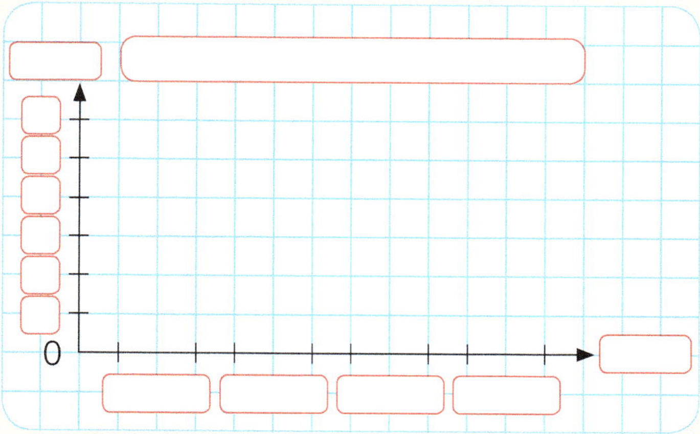

a. Who has the **most** points?

____

b. What is the difference, in points, between first and second place?

____

c. How many **more** points does third place need to reach first place?

____

2. Do you know what number Freddy will get? Explain.

____

____

____

____

The Survey

Connecting

Carl is conducting a survey to find out some information about his classmates.

conducting: organizing and carrying out

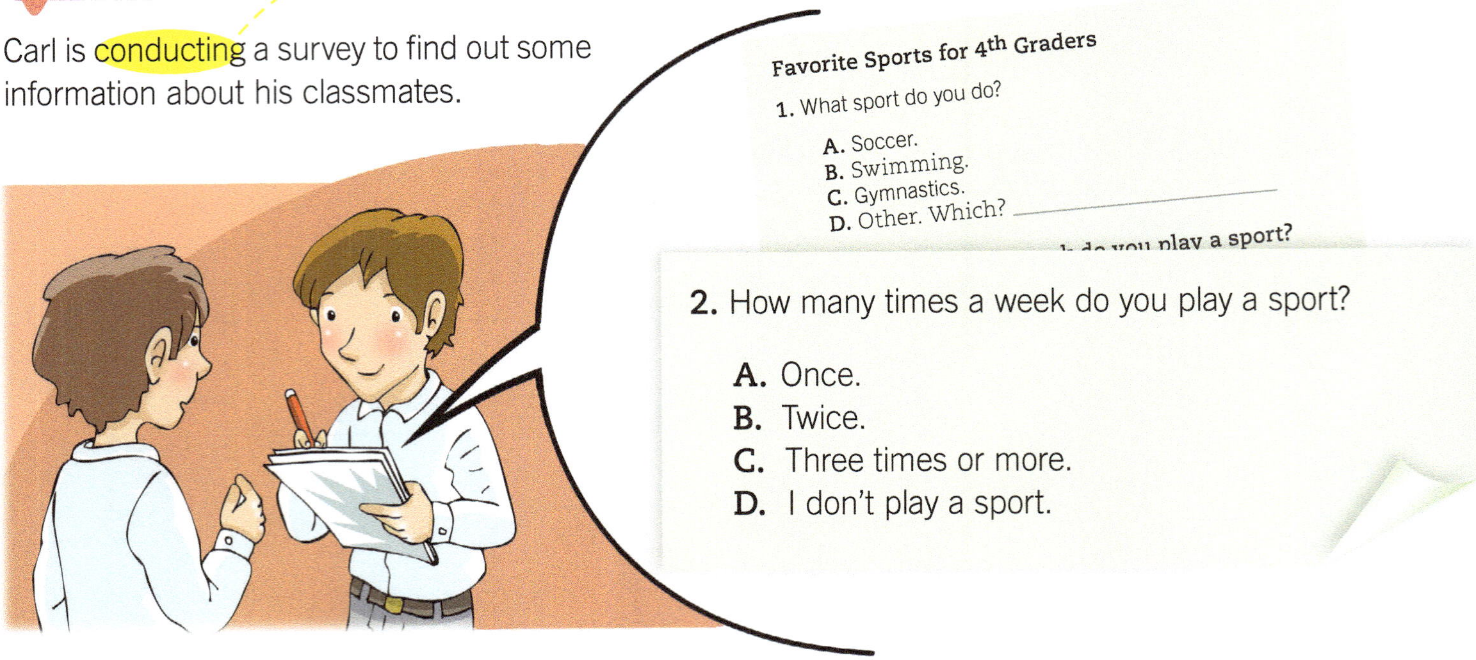

- What information will Carl obtain by asking the questions in his survey?

____

____

- Do you think the information will be useful? Explain.

____

____

- Will each person surveyed have the same answer to each question? Explain.

____

____

- What other question could be added to Carl's survey?

____

____

Learning

A **survey** is composed of simple **questions** that collect information or find out people's opinions on a certain subject.

Example:

To know what means of transportation students take to school, the following survey was conducted.

Means of Transportation to Get to School → Title explaining the objective of the survey.

1. How do you travel to school? → The question of the survey.

- **A.** By car.
- **B.** By bus.
- **C.** Walking.
- **D.** Other. How? ______________

→ Possible answers.

Practicing

1. Mark the question that gives you information about your classmates' favorite food with an ✕. Interpret

☐ What did you eat for lunch yesterday? ☐ What did you bring for lunch today?

☐ What food do you like the most? ☐ What food do you like the least?

2. Look at the following situation and answer. Analyze

Peter and Rachel are making a survey to find out what people do on *Earth Day*.

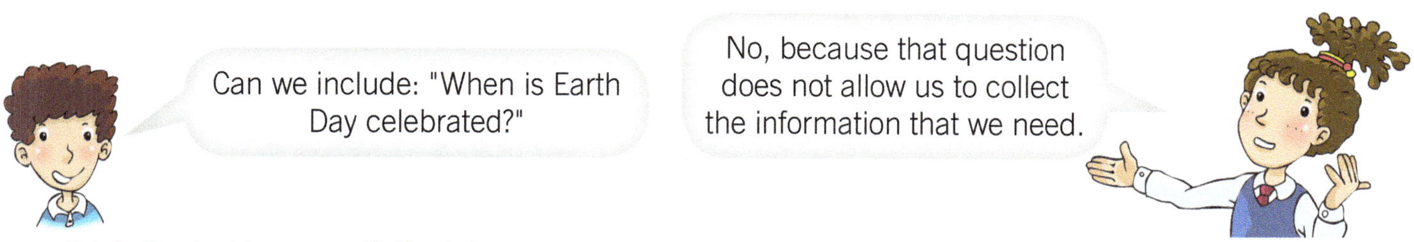

Do you think Rachel is correct? Explain.

____

Population and Samples

Connecting

Heather does not know which movie she is going to watch during Movie Week.

- Why do you think Heather will survey only 15 girls and not all of the girls in 4th grade?

- Why do you think Heather will only survey the girls from 4th grade and not those from 8th grade?

- If Heather surveys 15 boys from 4th grade, will she obtain the same results as if she surveyed 15 girls from 4th grade? Why or why not?

- If you prepared the question, who would you survey so that the results were useful for you?

Learning

In a survey, a **population** is the total set of people who have a common characteristic.

In many cases, it would be too expensive or take too much time to survey the entire population; therefore, only a portion of the population is surveyed. This portion is called a **sample**. When the people or things that compose a sample are selected randomly, we say that it is a **random sample**.

Practicing

1. In the following situations, indicate what the population is and choose a random sample that could represent that population. Understand

a. We want to find out what music young Canadians between the ages of 14 and 18 like.

Population ▶ ______________________

Sample ▶ ______________________

b. We want to find out what students in our school think about the school's dress code.

Population ▶ ______________________

Sample ▶ ______________________

Did You Know...?

A **sample** is representative if it is able to reproduce the characteristics of a population on a small scale.

serve as an example

2. Determine if the sample chosen is representative in each case. Analyze

a. Laura wants to find out what the most common means of transportation is. To do this, she will survey people randomly at a bus station. Is this sample the most appropriate?

(Yes) (No), because ______________________

____

b. Jason wanted to find out how many people go to the gym at least once a week. For this, he randomly surveyed people who were at the gym. Was the sample chosen by Jason the most appropriate?

(Yes) (No), because ______________________

____

Analyzing Survey Answers

Connecting

Brian surveyed his classmates to find out what their favorite fruits were.

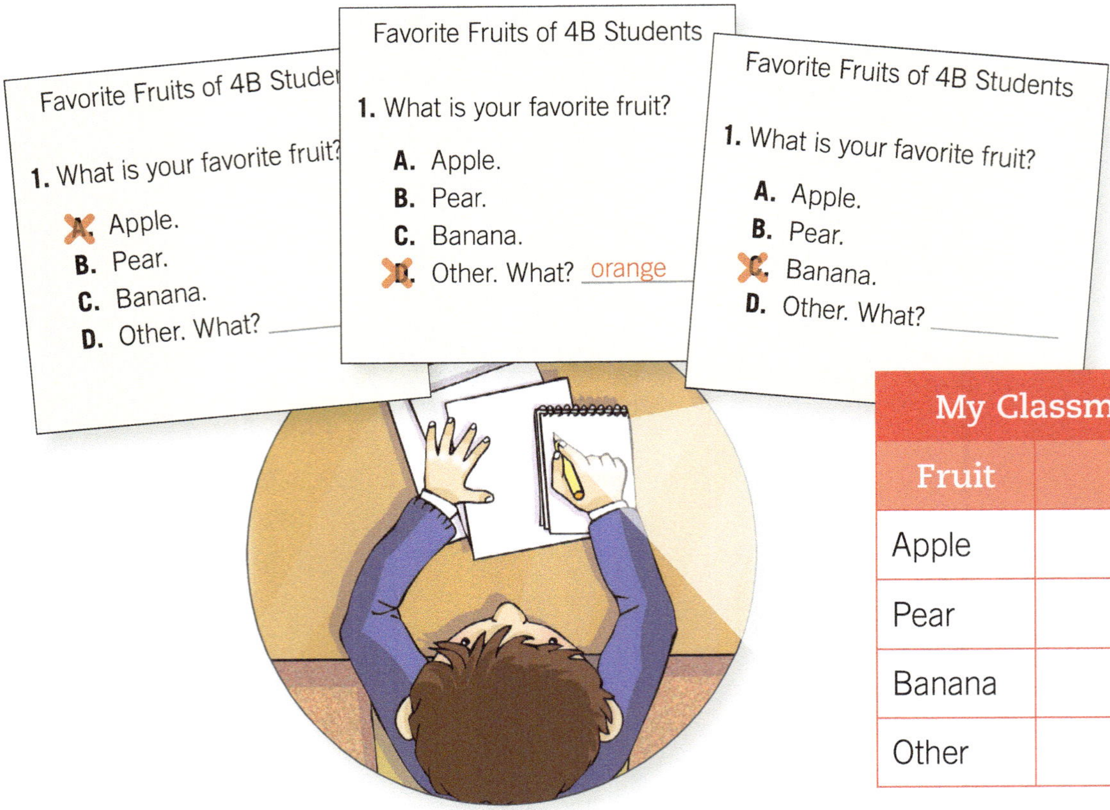

My Classmates' Favorite Fruit

Fruit	Tally	Total
Apple	卌 |||	8
Pear	卌	5
Banana	卌 ||||	9
Other	|||	3

- Why is it useful for Brian to record the answers in a table?

____

____

- What information can be obtained from the table?

____

____

- What other instrument can we use to organize the data obtained from the survey?

____

____

Learning

Survey data can be **recorded in a table or chart**. Then you can analyze the **results**.

Example:

The following chart shows the results obtained after surveying students in a 4th grade class about the number of pets they have.

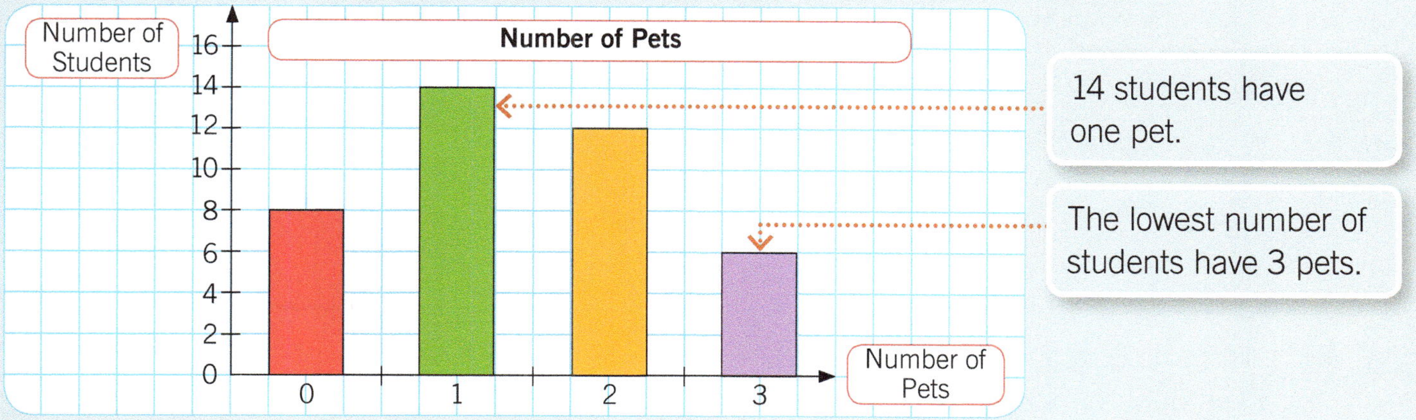

Practicing

1. Read the following situation and do the activity. Analyze

brothers or sisters

Some students in 4th grade were asked the following question: How many siblings do you have? The answers obtained were:

0, 1, 3, 2, 2, 3, 2, 4, 1, 2, 1, 2, 0, 2, 3, 1, 1, 0, 2, 4, 0, 1, 2, 3, 1, 1, 2, 2, 2

a. Make a simple bar chart with the results from the survey.

b. How many students have more than 3 siblings? ▶ ______

c. How many students in 4th grade do not have siblings? How do you know?

____

____

Quiz Yourself

Do the activity following the steps.

fun and relaxing

Step 1 Choose one of the topics.

☐ recreational activities ☐ outdoor games

Step 2 Write a survey title.

Title ▶ ______________________________

Step 3 Write two questions for the survey.
Each question should have 4 possible responses.

Question 1

____

______________________________?

A. ______________________________
B. ______________________________
C. ______________________________
D. ______________________________

Question 2

____

______________________________?

A. ______________________________
B. ______________________________
C. ______________________________
D. ______________________________

Step 4 Survey 10 of your classmates with the two questions. Complete.

Population ▶ ______________________________
Sample ▶ ______________________________

Step 5 Make a table and a simple bar chart with the results.

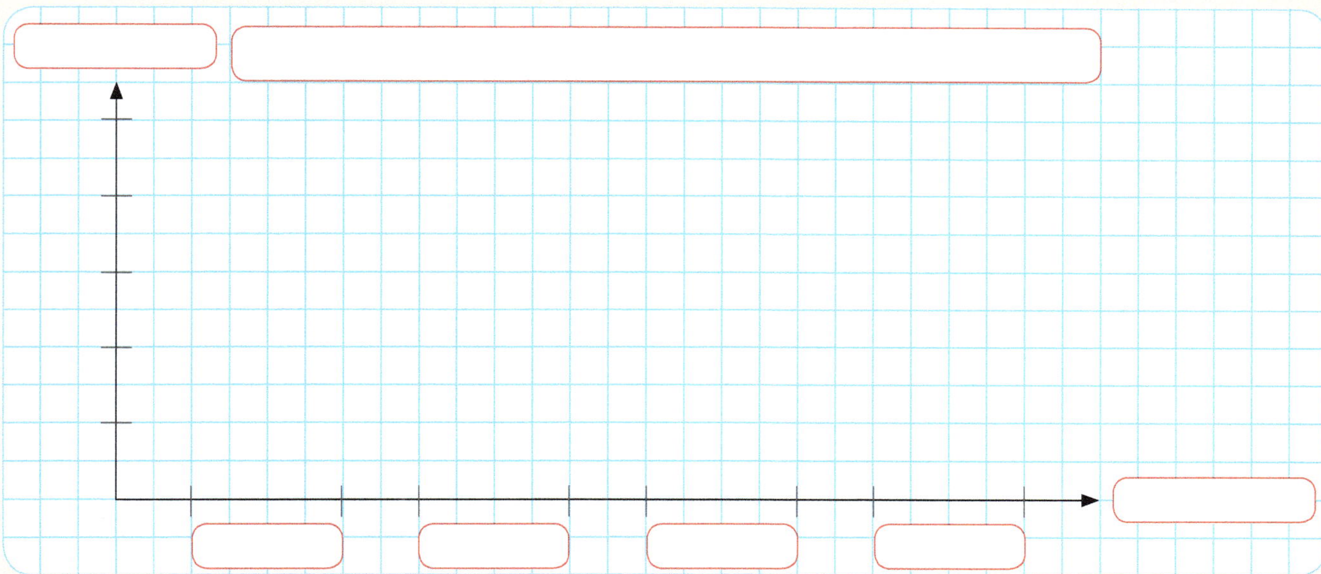

Step 6 Write three conclusions you can make from the information.

- ▶ ______________________________
- ▶ ______________________________
- ▶ ______________________________

Let's Check!

Analyzing Survey Answers

1. Look at the data in the table and answer.

points: ___ / 6

The following table shows the results of a survey of young adults and adults who live in Dallas.

Recreational Activities		
Type of Activity	People Surveyed	
	Young Adults	Adults
Reading	21	45
Going for Walks	35	24
Playing Sports	42	40
Listening to Music	36	15

a. What is the survey topic?

___

b. What do you think the survey question is?

___

c. What are the alternative responses to the question asked?

___

d. What is the population and sample of the survey?

Population ▶ ___

Sample ▶ ___

e. What were the most popular recreational activities for young adults and adults? Why do you think that is? Explain.

___

f. Which recreational activity had the biggest difference between young adults and adults? Why do you think that is? Explain.

___

Comparing Survey Answers

2. Read the following situation and answer.

The following charts were made based on answers from a survey.

How many siblings do you have?

A. 0.
B. 1, 2 or 3.
C. 4, 5 or 6.
D. More than 6.

points
3

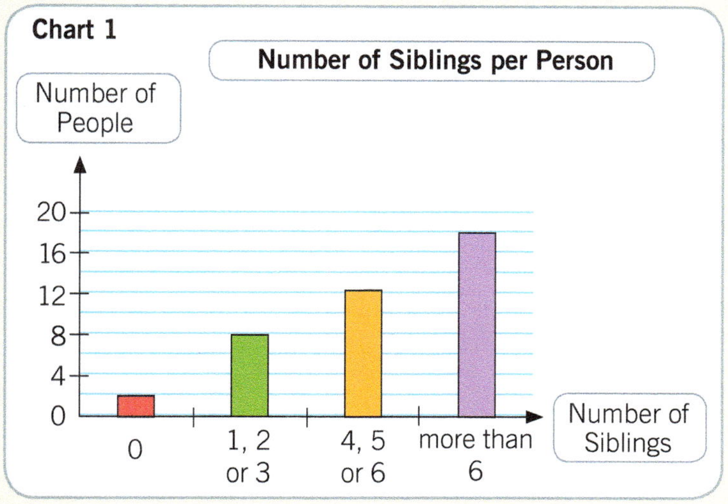

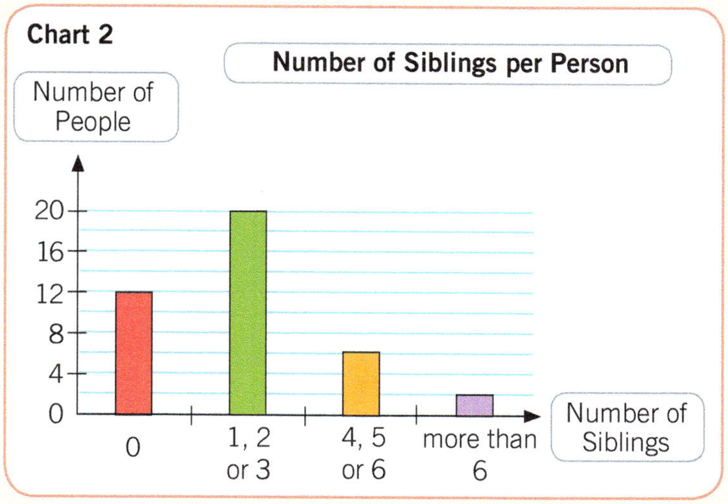

a. How many people were surveyed in each sample?

____

b. What differences can you see in the answers for each sample?

____

c. Who do you think was surveyed in each case? Explain.

Chart 1

____

____

Chart 2

____

____

Section 2

Pictographs and Simple Bar Charts

Reading and Interpreting Pictographs

Connecting

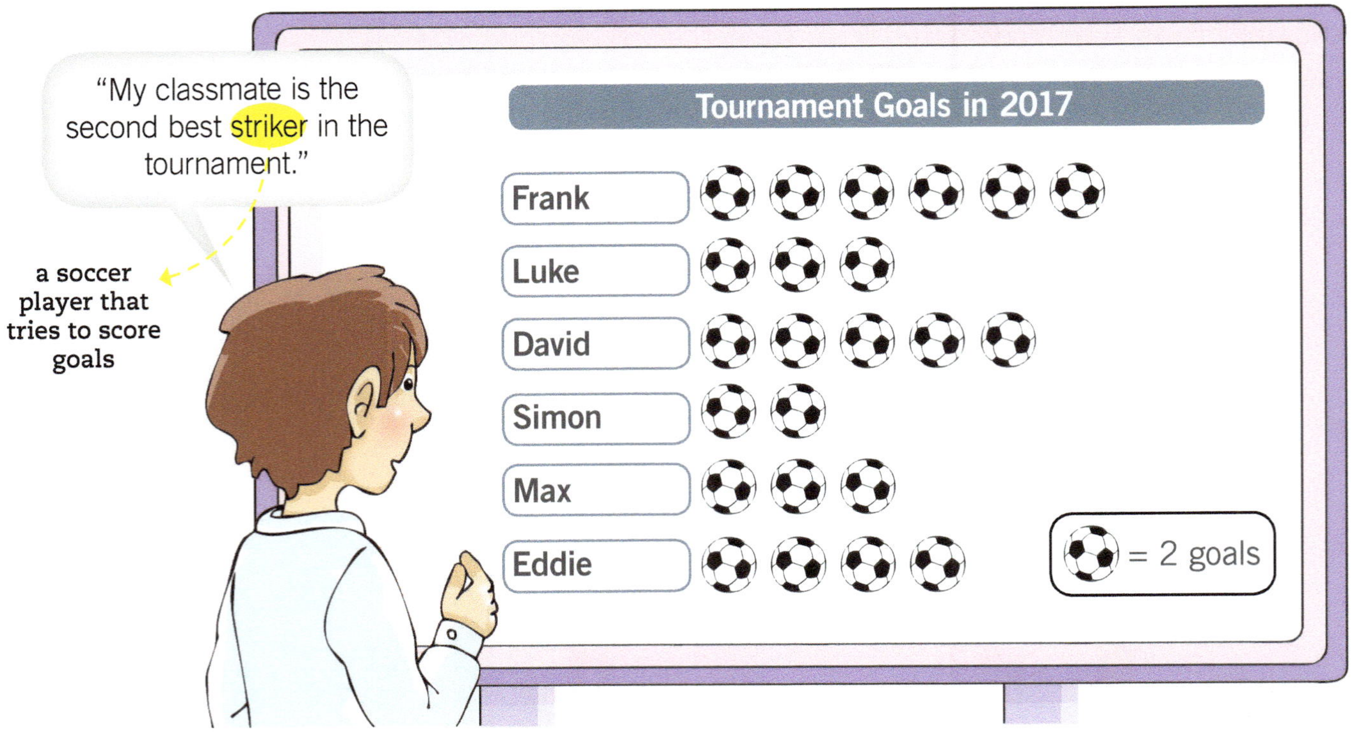

- Who is the boy's classmate? How do you know?

____

____

- Who has scored the most goals? Who has scored the least goals?

____

____

- If the tournament ended with these results, who would win 1st, 2nd and 3rd place?

1st place ▶ _______ **2nd place** ▶ _______ **3rd place** ▶ _______

Learning

A **pictograph** allows us to organize information in a clear and precise way, making it easier to **read** and **interpret**.

Example:

This pictograph represents the number of hours children watch TV, Friday through Sunday.

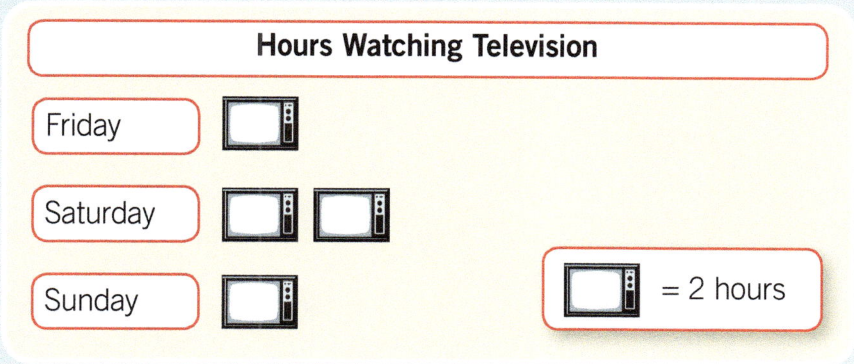

Some interpretations we can draw are that:

- children watch more television on Saturdays.
- children watch 6 hours of television between Saturday and Sunday.

Practicing

1. Look at the pictograph and write two conclusions. Interpret

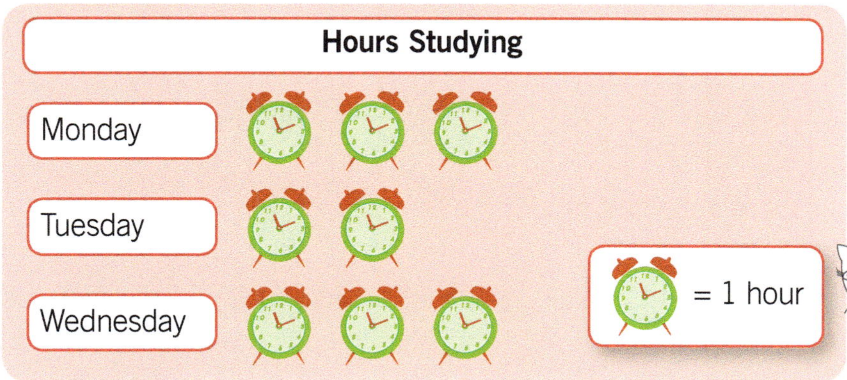

Conclusion 1 ▶ ______________________________

Conclusion 2 ▶ ______________________________

2. Look at the pictograph and answer. Analyze

In May, students decided to have a book collection to help schools with less resources.

a. What grades participated in the campaign?

b. Do you know how many classes from each grade participated in the campaign? Explain.

c. How many books did each grade collect?

1st Grade ▶ ☐ 2nd Grade ▶ ☐

3rd Grade ▶ ☐ 4th Grade ▶ ☐

d. How many books were collected in all? ▶ ☐

e. Why do you think the students chose to collect books in May? Write two possible reasons.

Reason 1 ▶

Reason 2 ▶

3. Look at the pictograph and answer. Analyze

The school librarian did an inventory of the books in the library.

a complete list of items

a. How many books of each type are there?

Children's ▶ ☐ Science Fiction ▶ ☐

Novels ▶ ☐ Nonfiction ▶ ☐

b. How many books are there in the library in all? ▶ ☐

c. What type of book is there the most of? Why do you think there are so many of these types of books?

____

____

d. Which type of book do you think is the most popular? Explain.

____

____

Reading and Interpreting Simple Bar Charts

Connecting

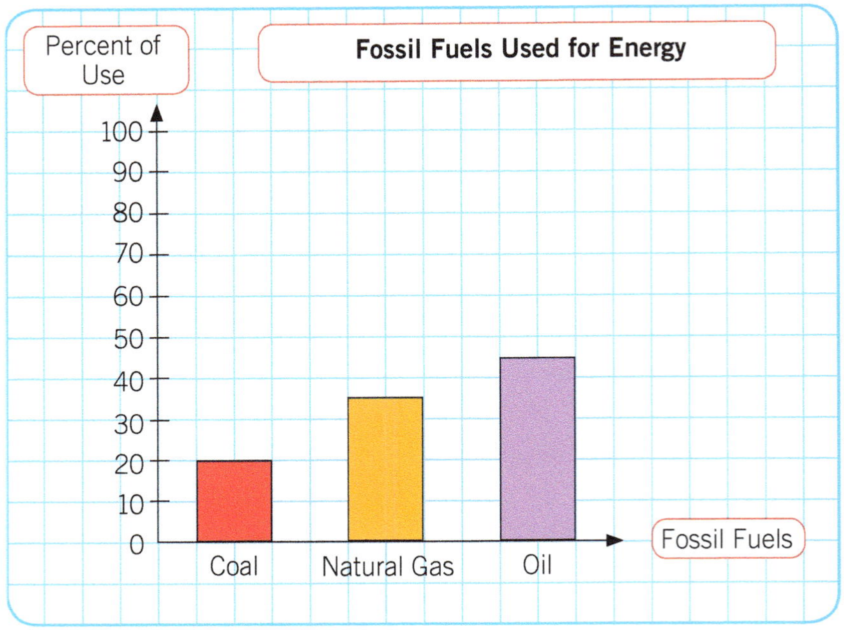

- What information is represented in the chart?

____

____

- Which fossil fuel is used the most? Which one is used the least?

____

____

Education through Values

Renewable energy comes from the sun, wind, ocean tides and heat inside the Earth. If countries used more of these sources and less fossil fuels, our air and planet would be cleaner.

Learning

To **read and interpret a simple bar chart**, first you must look at the axes and then the quantities represented.

Example:

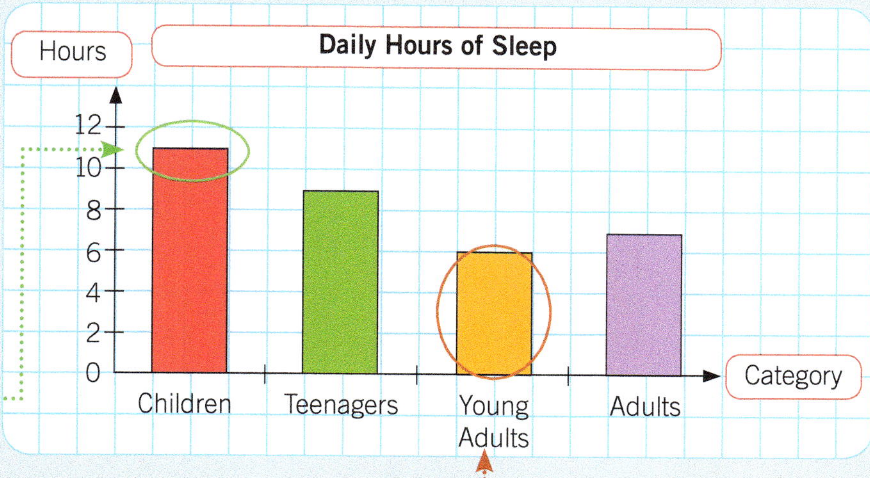

From this chart you can read and interpret that:

- children sleep approximately 11 hours daily.
- young adults sleep less hours daily.

Practicing

1. Look at the chart and answer. Interpret

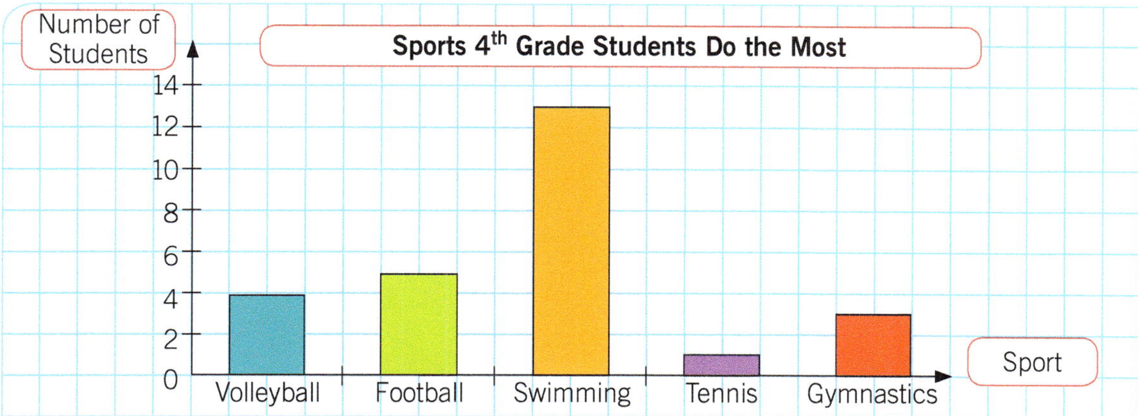

a. What information does the chart represent? ____________________

____

b. Which sport do the students do the **most**? ____________________

____

c. Which sport do the students do the **least**? ____________________

2. Look at the following chart and answer. Analyze

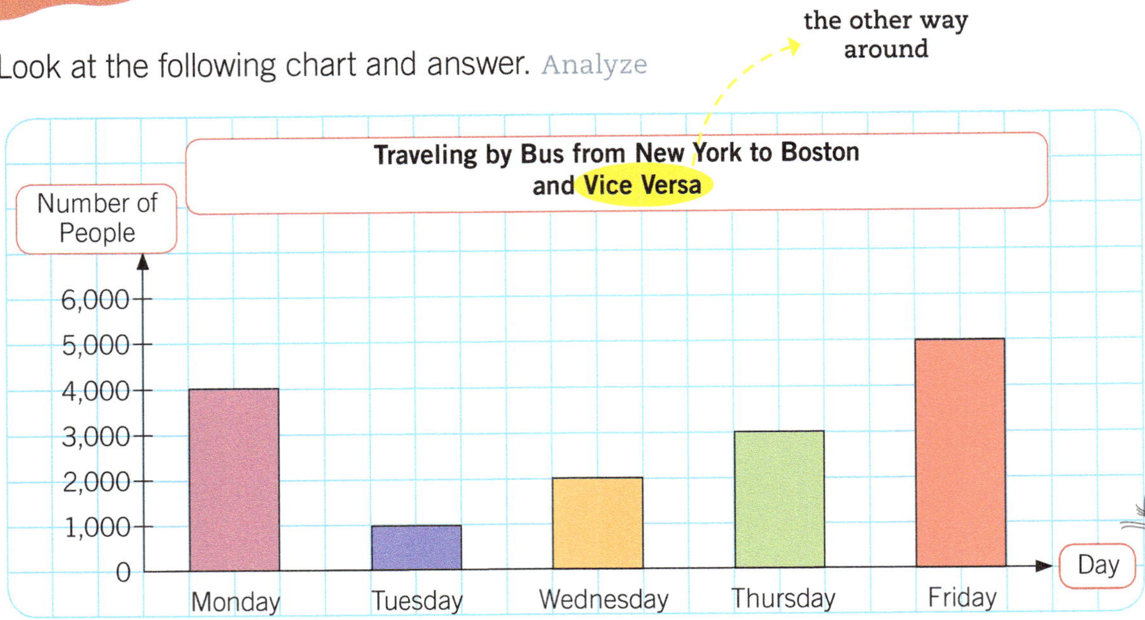

a. What information is represented in the chart?

____

____

b. How many people travel each day?

Monday ▶ ☐ Wednesday ▶ ☐ Friday ▶ ☐

Tuesday ▶ ☐ Thursday ▶ ☐

c. On which day do people travel the least?

____

d. Why do you think people travel the most on Monday and Friday?

____

____

e. Can you obtain information about the number of people that travel on Saturday and Sunday?

____

____

Quiz Yourself

Read the situation and answer.

Phillip found an electric bill, and he was interested in the bar chart that was on it.

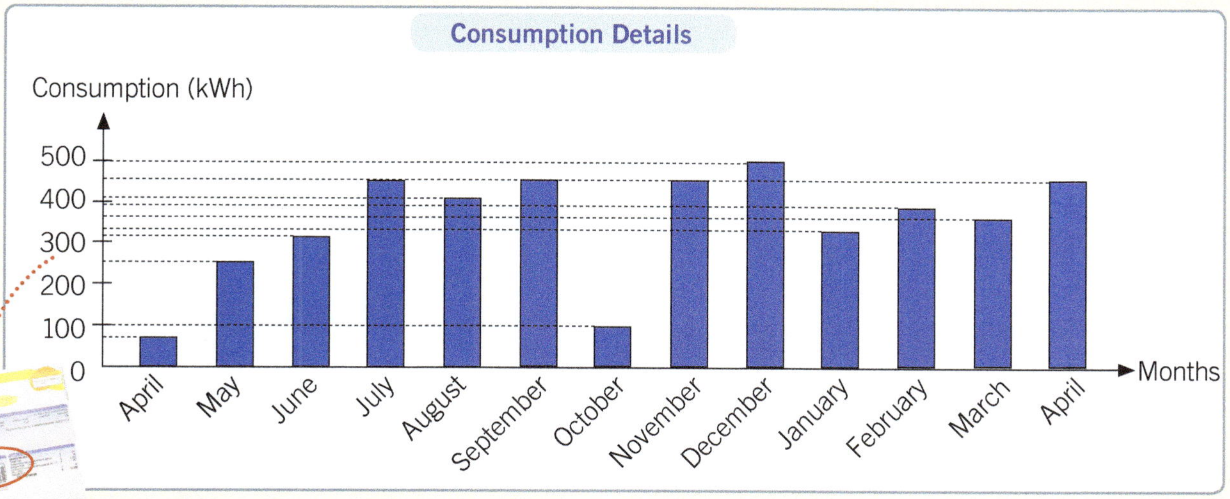

- What information is represented in the chart?

Did You Know...?

The consumption of electricity is measured in **kilowatts** per hour. The abbreviation for kilowatts per hour is **kWh**.

- How many months of energy consumption are represented in the chart? How much time is that equal to?

- Consumption was the **greatest** in which month? Why do you think that was?

Quiz Yourself

Do the following activity with a classmate.

Step 1 Cut out the cards on **Activity Card 1** and put them in a bag.

Step 2 Without looking, take a card and record its color in the tally column.
Then put the card back into the bag.
Repeat 15 times, making sure to take turns taking out the cards.

Step 3 Make a bar chart with the results and answer.

Results of Picking a Colored Card		
Color	Tally	Total
Red		
Blue		
Green		

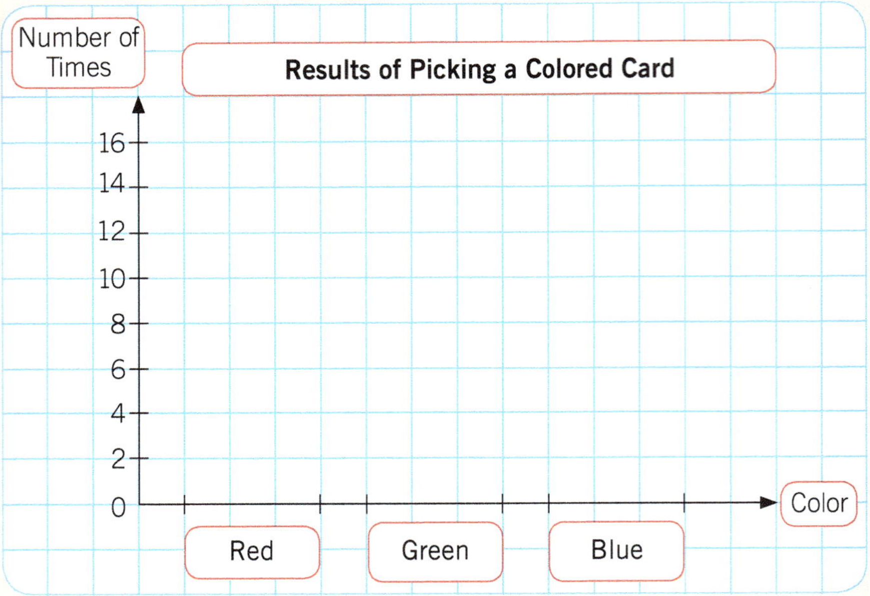

a. Which color was picked the most?

____

b. Which color was picked the least? How would you know by looking only at the bar chart?

____

____

c. Is it possible to find out how many times a yellow card was picked? Explain.

____

____

Exam Strategies

Multiple-Choice Questions

1. Look at the information presented on the pictograph. In all, how many cell phones were sold during the three months?

A. 10 cell phones
B. 30 cell phones
C. 40 cell phones
D. 300 cell phones

Analyzing the Answers

A. In this case, the images have been counted for each month. It has not been taken into consideration that each image represents 30 cell phones.

$$3 + 5 + 2 = 10$$

B. In this case, the cell phones have been counted for each month, but there has been a mistake in the multiplication of phones. The symbol was mistakenly thought to represent 3 phones rather than 30 cell phones.

$$10 \times 3 = 30$$

C. In this case, the cell phones have been counted for each month, but instead of multiplying them, they have been added.

$$10 + 30 = 40$$

D. The total number of cell phones sold has been counted, and the correct scale has been applied.

$$10 \times 30 = 300$$

▸ Therefore, the correct answer is **D.**

1. A — B — C — D

What Did You Learn?

Final Evaluation

1. Choose one of the topics and make a survey with two questions.

points
___ / 4

☐ TV Programs ☐ Animals ☐ Healthy Eating

Title: ____________________

1. ____?
   a. ____________________
   b. ____________________
   c. ____________________
2. ____?
   a. ____________________
   b. ____________________
   c. ____________________

2. Identify the population and sample for each of the situations.

points
___ / 4

a. The student council wants to know what music students like. To do this, they randomly surveyed 10 students from each class.

Population ▶ ____________________

Sample ▶ ____________________

b. A study wants to know how much money an average Australian family spends during a whole week on public transportation. They surveyed 50 families from each region of the country.

Population ▶ ____________________

Sample ▶ ____________________

3. Do the following activities based on the information in the table.

points

/ 4

4th Grade Students' Favorite Juice	
Juice	**Votes**
Apple	20
Orange	45
Grape	30
Strawberry	40

a. Make a bar chart with the information above.

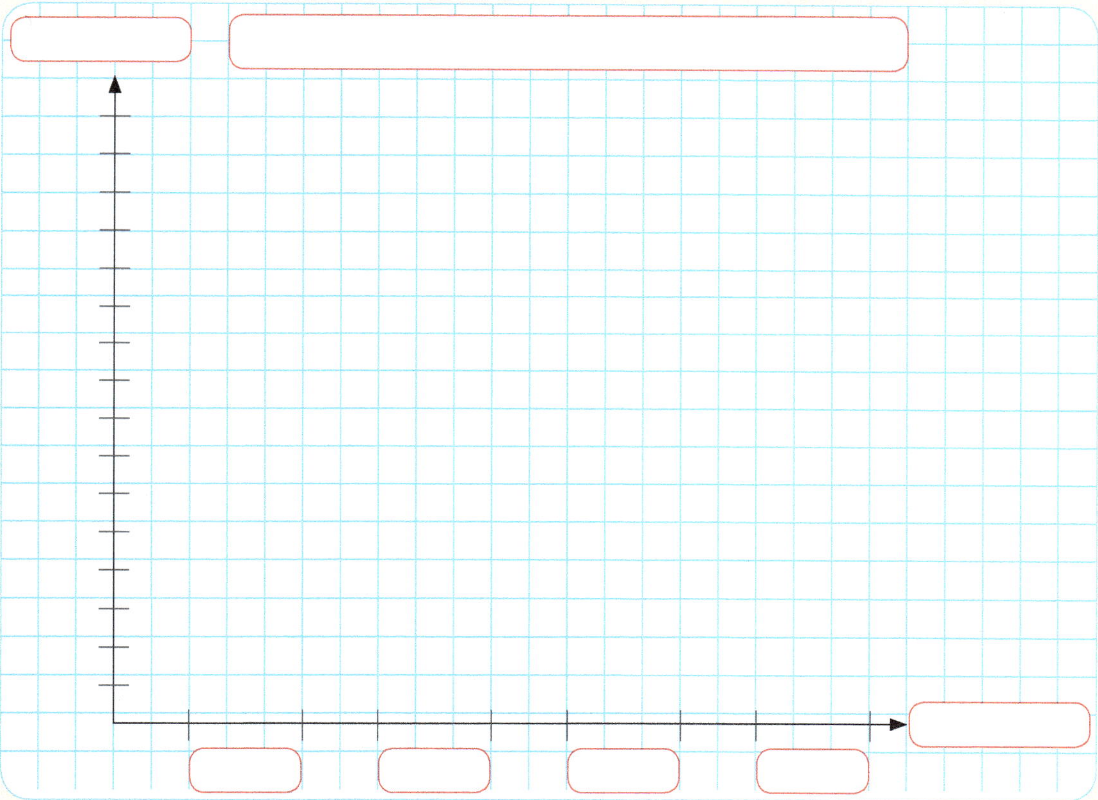

b. What information does the chart give us?

____

c. Which option is the most popular?

____

d. How many **more** votes did orange juice get compared to grape juice?

____

4. Look at the following information and answer.

points ⁄ 4

The charts show the survey answers of men and women.

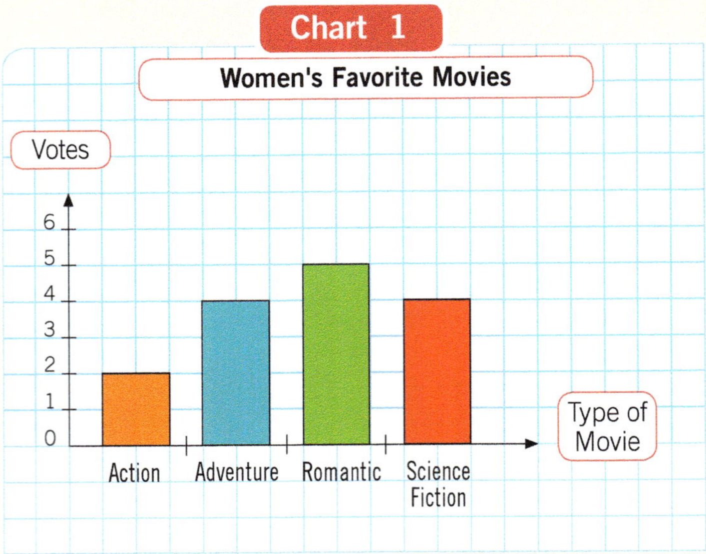

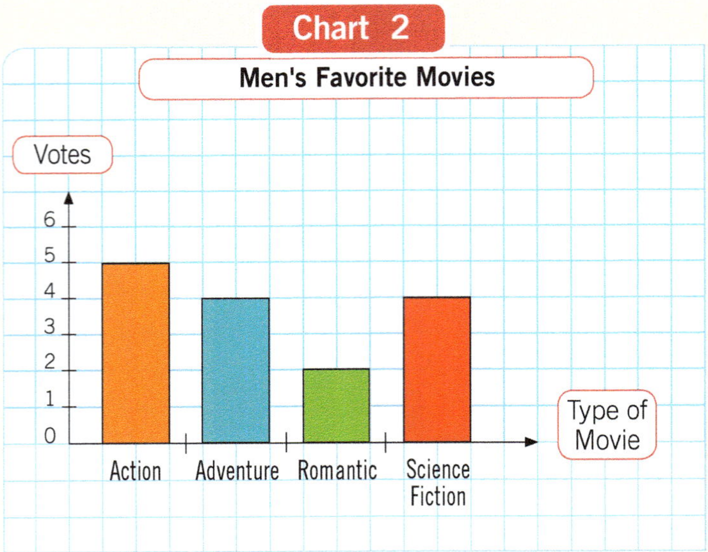

a. Which type of movie was the most popular for each group?

Chart 1 ▶ ______________________________

Chart 2 ▶ ______________________________

b. How many people were surveyed for each group?

Chart 1 ▶ ______________________________

Chart 2 ▶ ______________________________

Mark the correct answer with an ✖.

points

/ 3

Look at the following chart and answer **questions 5–7**.

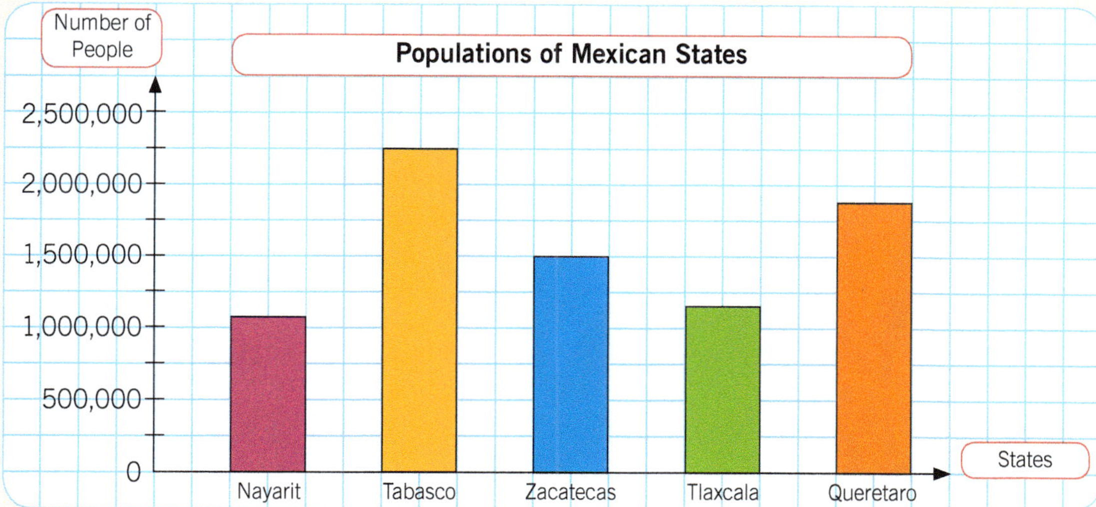

5. Which state has the most people?

A. Nayarit

B. Tabasco

C. Zacatecas

D. Queretaro

6. Approximately how many people does Zacatecas have?

A. 2,000,000 people

B. 2,500,000 people

C. 1,500,000 people

D. 1,000,000 people

7. Which state has the least number of people?

A. Nayarit

B. Tabasco

C. Zacatecas

D. Queretaro

Find Test 2 Study page.

Unit 3 Numbers Up To 1,000,000

Key Words

million

interval

In this unit you will learn to:

- read, write and represent numbers up to 1,000,000.
- compose and decompose numbers up to 1,000,000.
- compare and put numbers up to 1,000,000 in order.
- have a positive attitude and trust your math skills.

What Do You Know? Initial Evaluation

Look at the image and answer.

1. Write the price of one of the bicycles in word form.

____

2. How much money would the family spend on the cheapest computer and the cheapest stuffed animal?

cheapest → that costs the least money

3. How much more would they pay for the teddy bear than for the stuffed duck?

4. How much money is needed to buy the most expensive computer and the cheapest bicycle?

Numbers Up To 1,000,000

Hundred Thousands and a Million

Connecting

The 4th grade math teacher asked her students to write an unknown number with 6 digits. A 0 is in both the ones and thousands place. There is a 7 that has a place value of 700,000 and another one with a place value of 700. The other digits have a place value of 60 and 30,000.

- Help Claire find the unknown number.

Learning

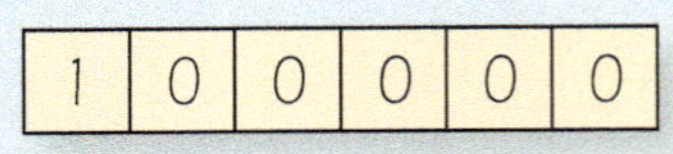

million

hundred thousand

One **million** is equal to

- ten hundred thousands.
- one hundred ten thousands.
- one thousand thousands.

When writing numbers, the comma separates the O, T, H from the thousands family, Th, TTh, HTh and the millions family, M, TM, HM.

Example:

658,658 is read six hundred fifty-eight thousand, six hundred fifty-eight.

1,000,000 is read as one million.

Practicing

1. Look at the numbers and write how many hundred thousands are needed to make one million. Apply

a.

HTh	TTh	Th	H	T	O
5	0	0	0	0	0

needs ________ **HTh** to make a million.

b.

HTh	TTh	Th	H	T	O
8	0	0	0	0	0

needs ________ **HTh** to make a million.

c.

HTh	TTh	Th	H	T	O
2	0	0	0	0	0

needs ________ **HTh** to make a million.

2. Complete the equivalencies with the correct number. Apply

a.

HTh	TTh	Th	H	T	O
3	5	0	8	0	0

equals [ ] **O.**

b.

HTh	TTh	Th	H	T	O
5	2	0	0	0	0

equals [ ] **Th.**

c.

HTh	TTh	Th	H	T	O
2	8	1	4	0	0

equals [ ] **H.**

Did You Know...?

People often use the word "million" as an exaggeration of something that is a large amount! Write a few sentences using the word million as an exaggeration.

3. Match each number with its word form. Relate

a. 460,920

b. 940,500

c. 406,920

d. 904,500

- four hundred six thousand, nine hundred twenty
- four hundred sixty thousand, nine hundred twenty
- nine hundred four thousand, five hundred
- nine hundred forty thousand, five hundred

Place Value

Connecting

Thomas is analyzing the numbers that the teacher placed on the board.

- What is similar about the numbers?

____

- What digit is in the hundred thousands place in each number? What value does it have?

  In the number 793,501, the digit in the **HTh** place is ______ and has a value of ______.

  In the number 709,153, the digit in the **HTh** place is ______ and has a value of ______.

- If you only consider the **HTh** place, can you know which number is greater? Explain.

____

- What digits are in the ten thousands place in the numbers? What value do they have?

  In the number 793,501, the digit in the **TTh** place is ______ and has a value of ______.

  In the number 709,153, the digit in the **TTh** place is ______ and has a value of ______.

- If you only consider the **TTh** place, will you know which number is greater? Explain.

____

- If you compare two numbers with the same number of digits, how do you know which one is greater? Explain.

____

____

Learning

Remember, the **value** of digits depends on their **position** in a number.

Example:

The numbers 908,000 and 890,000 are made with the same digits but represent different quantities because the digits are in different positions.

908,000					
HTh	TTh	Th	H	T	O
9	0	8	0	0	0

890,000					
HTh	TTh	Th	H	T	O
8	9	0	0	0	0

The number 9 in 908,000 has a **place value** of **900,000** in the **HTh** place.
in 890,000 has a **place value** of **90,000** in the **TTh** place.

The number 8 in 908,000 has a **place value** of **8,000** in the **Th** place.
in 890,000 has a **place value** of **800,000** in the **HTh** place.

Practicing

1. Circle the numbers in which the digit 5 has a place value **greater than** 500. Identify

590,749 609,563 350,319 160,359

592,829 495,290 206,510 793,005

2. Look at the highlighted digit and match it to its correct place value. Relate

a. 371,378

b. 276,029

c. 714,395

d. 527,362

700,000

70,000

7,000

700

70

7

Composing and Decomposing Numbers

Connecting

The students just finished playing a board game and are counting their money like this:

- What does **$10,000** ▸ 𝍸 𝍸 || mean?

____

- How can you represent, with multiplication, the amount of money collected in $10,000 bills? ▸ ☐ × ☐

- How much money was collected? How do you know?

____

____

____

____

Education through Values

Playing board games is a great way to spend time with your family and friends. It's also a nice break from staring at a screen.

Learning

You can **compose** a number by writing each digit in the correct position according to its place value.

Example:

1 hundred thousand, 2 ten thousands, 8 thousands, 5 hundreds, 9 tens and 4 ones

1 **HTh** + 2 **TTh** + 8 **Th** + 5 **H** + 9 **T** + 4 **O**

100,000 + 20,000 + 8,000 + 500 + 90 + 4

128,594

You can **decompose** a number by writing the place value of each digit of the number or the position of the digits.

Example:

258,476

200,000 + 50,000 + 8,000 + 400 + 70 + 6

2 **HTh** + 5 **TTh** + 8 **Th** + 4 **H** + 7 **T** + 6 **O**

2 hundred thousands, 5 ten thousands, 8 thousands, 4 hundreds, 7 tens and 6 ones

Practicing

1. Write the decomposition of each number. Apply

a. 596,283

_______ **HTh** + _______ **TTh** + _______ **Th** + _______ **H** + _______ **T** + _______ **O**

_______ + _______ + _______ + _______ + _______ + _______

b. 974,174

_______ **HTh** + _______ **TTh** + _______ **Th** + _______ **H** + _______ **T** + _______ **O**

_______ + _______ + _______ + _______ + _______ + _______

c. 295,603

_______ **HTh** + _______ **TTh** + _______ **Th** + _______ **H** + _______ **T** + _______ **O**

_______ + _______ + _______ + _______ + _______ + _______

2. Complete the table with the composition or decomposition of numbers. Apply

Composition	Decomposition Using Digit Position	Decomposition Using Place Value
	4 **HTh** + 6 **TTh** + 2 **Th** + 7 **T** + 2 **O**	
		300,000 + 6,000 + 300 + 90
	2 **HTh** + 2 **TTh** + 3 **H** + 6 **T** + 9 **O**	
683,194		
		100,000 + 20,000 + 6,000 + 200 + 5

3. Compose the numbers. Apply

a. 400,000 + 80,000 + 2,000 + 300 + 40 + 1 ▶ ______

b. 8 **HTh** + 3 **TTh** + 4 **Th** + 5 **H** + 8 **T** + 3 **O** ▶ ______

c. 500,000 + 10,000 + 3,000 + 40 + 5 ▶ ______

d. 7 **HTh** + 9 **TTh**+ 9 **H** + 4 **T** + 7 **O** ▶ ______

Fun Fact!

A million seconds equals 11.57 days!

4. Look at the situation and answer. Analyze

a. What number can be formed with the cards? ▶ ______

b. What did you do to make the number? Explain.

______

______

Quiz Yourself

Complete the number puzzle using the key.

Key

- **A** ▶ 8 **HTh** + 2 **Tth** + 9 **Th** + 8 **T** + 3 **O**
- **B** ▶ 900,000 + 70,000 + 3,000 + 500 + 80 + 6
- **C** ▶ 6 **HTh** + 2 **TTh** + 3 **Th** + 2 **H** + 9 **T** + 4 **O**
- **D** ▶ 300,000 + 10,000 + 1,000 + 400 + 20 + 4
- **E** ▶ 5 **HTh** + 1 **TTh** + 3 **Th** + 7 **H** + 2 **T** + 4 **O**
- **F** ▶ 200,000 + 60,000 + 200 + 70 + 5
- **G** ▶ 1 **HTh** + 6 **TTh** + 9 **Th** + 7 **H** + 8 **T** + 1 **O**
- **H** ▶ 400,000 + 30,000 + 2,000 + 100 + 7

Challenge

Sudoku is a type of **number puzzle**. Research these types of puzzles and try to solve one.

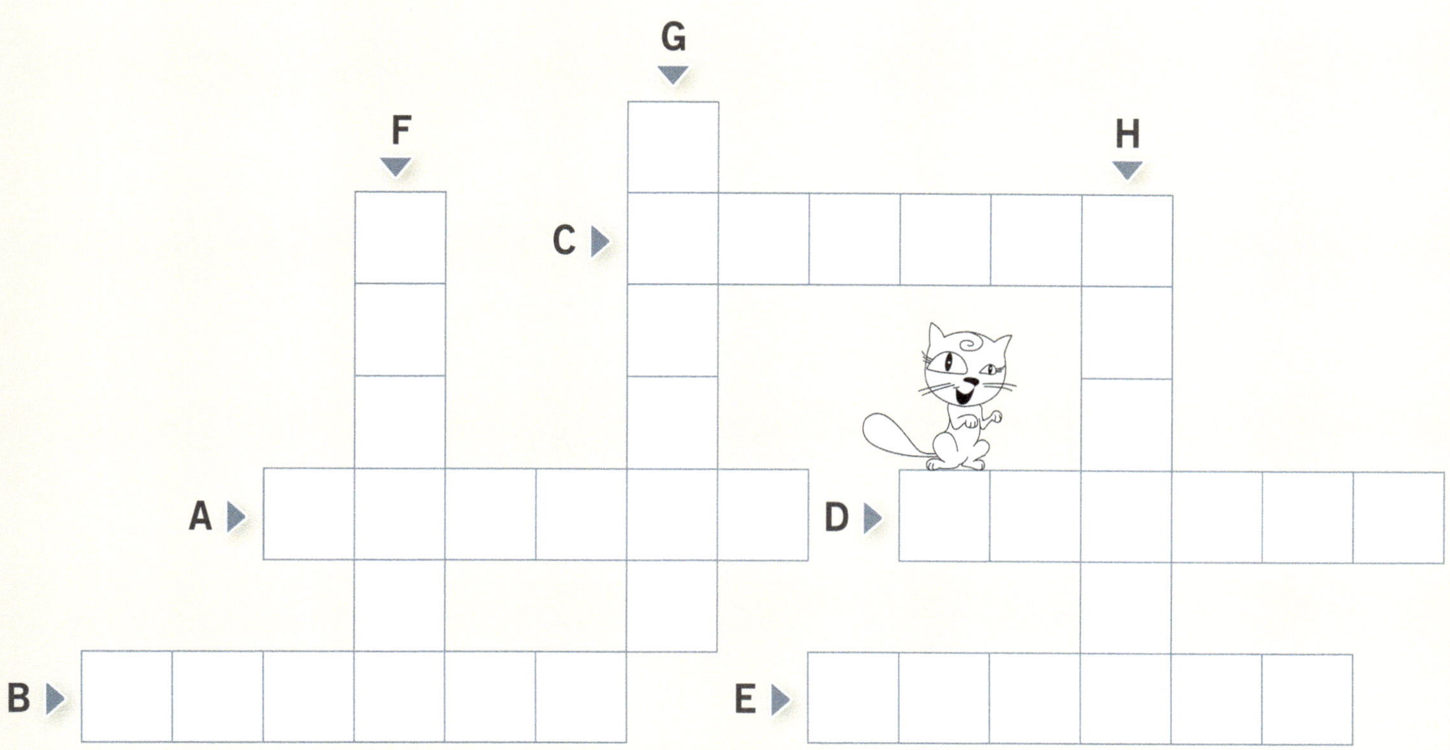

Comparing and Putting Numbers in Order Using a Place Value Chart

Connecting

- If both cost the same, why do you think Robert wants to buy the LIVE television?

____

____

- Which number position helped them determine the longer TV life span? Explain.

____

____

Learning

To **compare** numbers with the **same number of digits**, you can use a **place value chart**. Using this chart, place values of digits can be compared, from left to right, digit by digit.

Example:

HTh	TTh	Th	H	T	O
5	2	4	0	0	0

HTh	TTh	Th	H	T	O
5	4	2	0	0	0

500,000 = 500,000

20,000 < 40,000

20,000 is 20,000 ones less in 40,000.

524,000 is **less than** 542,000.

542,000 is **greater than** 524,000.

Practicing

1. Place the numbers in the place value chart. Compare them by writing >, < or =. Apply

a. 839,249 ◯ 859,302

HTh	TTh	Th	H	T	O

HTh	TTh	Th	H	T	O

b. 400,280 ◯ 300,900

HTh	TTh	Th	H	T	O

HTh	TTh	Th	H	T	O

c. 690,280 ◯ 690,350

HTh	TTh	Th	H	T	O

HTh	TTh	Th	H	T	O

2. Compare the numbers and circle the correct answer. Apply

a. The greater number.

HTh	TTh	Th	H	T	O
6	9	1	6	0	0

HTh	TTh	Th	H	T	O
6	9	3	7	0	0

b. The smaller number.

HTh	TTh	Th	H	T	O
2	7	0	4	2	5

HTh	TTh	Th	H	T	O
3	8	0	3	4	9

c. The smaller number.

HTh	TTh	Th	H	T	O
1	0	3	2	9	4

HTh	TTh	Th	H	T	O
1	9	3	5	0	0

Comparing and Putting Numbers in Order on a Number Line

Connecting

Nina put some numbers in order on a number line:

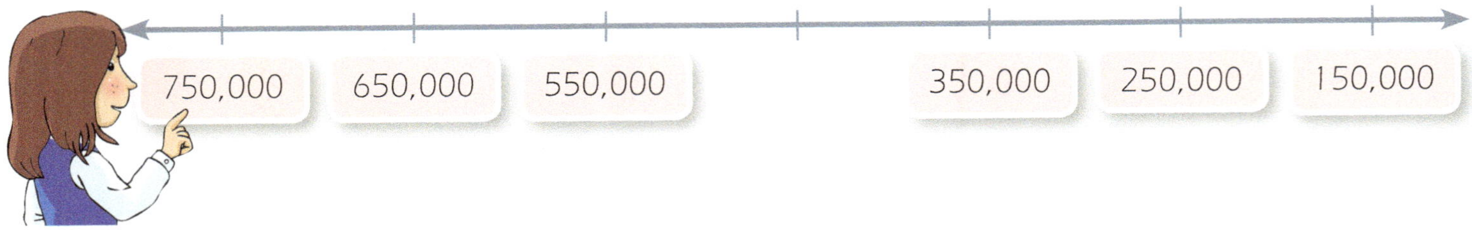

- What intervals is the number line divided into?

____

- Did Nina organize the numbers correctly? Explain.

(Yes) (No), because ____

____

- How should she have placed the numbers on the number line?

____

Learning

To **compare and put numbers** in order, a **number line** can be used.
A number is **less than** another number if it is located more toward the left on a number line.
A number is **greater than** another number if it is located more toward the right on a number line.

Example:

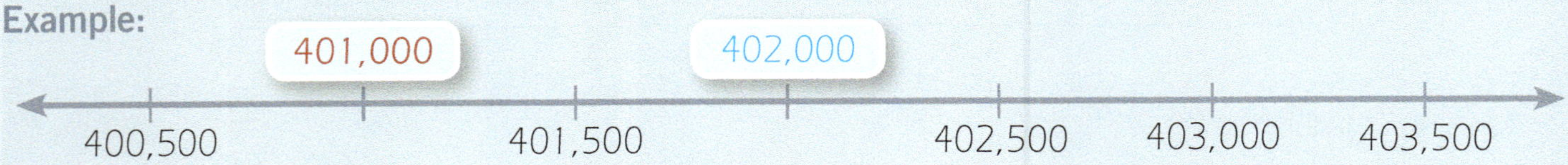

401,000 is to the left of 401,500 and is 500 less. ▶ 401,000 < 401,500

402,000 is to the right of 401,500 and is 500 greater. ▶ 402,000 > 401,500

Therefore, 401,000 < 402,000.

Practicing

1. Place the numbers on the number line. Represent

a. 670,000 470,000 270,000 370,000 570,000 170,000

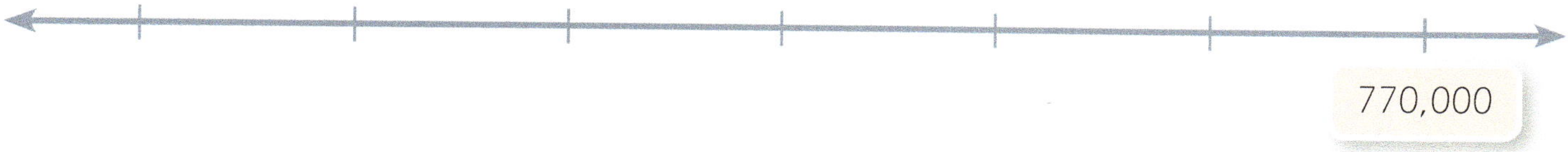

Smallest number ▶ ______ Greatest number ▶ ______

b. 955,000 930,000 935,000 945,000 950,000 940,000

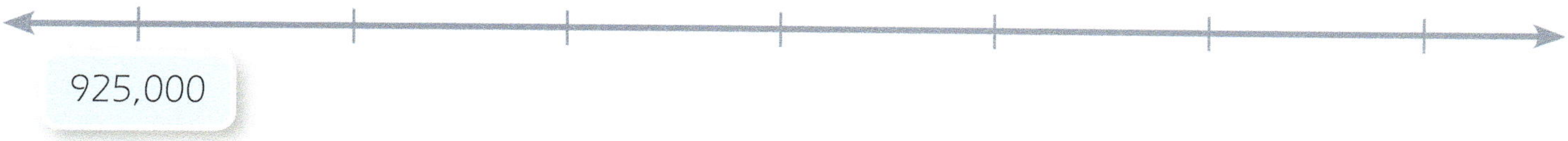

Smallest number ▶ ______ Greatest number ▶ ______

Quiz Yourself

Complete.

a. Compare the numbers 952,000, 951,200 and 951,500 using the place value chart. Then compare using >, < or =.

HTh	TTh	Th	H	T	O	HTh	TTh	Th	H	T	O	HTh	TTh	Th	H	T	O

______ ◯ ______ ◯ ______

b. Place the previous numbers on the number line.

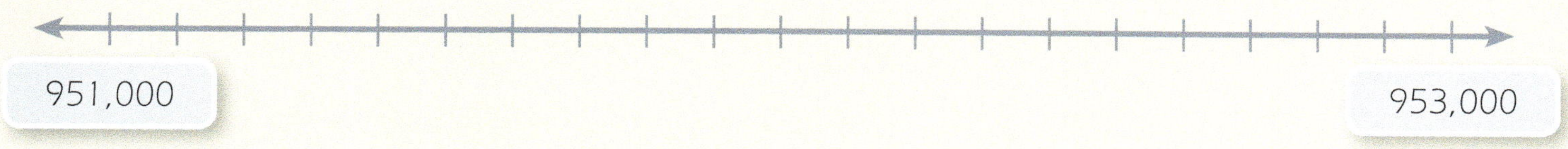

Let's Check!

Hundred Thousands

1. Write the following numbers in word form.

points: ___ / 3

a. 395,264 ▶ ____

____

b. 802,562 ▶ ____

____

c. 158,485 ▶ ____

____

Place Value

2. Complete, using the highlighted number.

points: ___ / 5

	Number	Position	Place Value
a.	682,394		
b.	195,965		
c.	710,003		
d.	449,285		
e.	663,872		

Composing and Decomposing Numbers

3. Complete with the composition or decomposition of the numbers.

points: ___ / 4

a. 395,284 ▶ _____ **HTh** + _____ **TTh** + _____ **Th** + _____ **H** + _____ **T** + _____ **O**

b. 890,672 ▶ __________ + __________ + __________ + __________ + __________

c. 4 **HTh** + 5 **TTh** + 6 **Th** + 1 **H** + 9 **T** + 5 **O** ▶ ______

d. 800,000 + 20,000 + 4,000 + 200 + 60 + 1 ▶ ______

Comparing and Putting Numbers in Order on a Place Value Chart

4. Compare. Then write >, < or =.

points __ / 3

a.

HTh	TTh	Th	H	T	O
6	9	0	5	2	8

◯

HTh	TTh	Th	H	T	O
6	0	9	5	2	8

b.

HTh	TTh	Th	H	T	O
9	9	3	5	3	3

◯

HTh	TTh	Th	H	T	O
9	9	3	5	4	9

c.

HTh	TTh	Th	H	T	O
5	2	6	2	6	2

◯

HTh	TTh	Th	H	T	O
5	2	6	2	6	2

Comparing and Putting Numbers in Order on a Number Line

5. Put the numbers in order on the number line and answer.

points __ / 2

a. 290,600 290,800 290,200 289,600

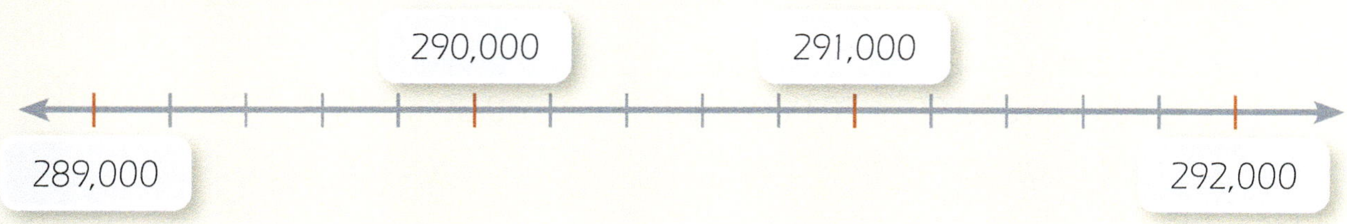

Which is the greatest number? ▶ ______

b. 876,391 879,391 877,391 875,391 872,391

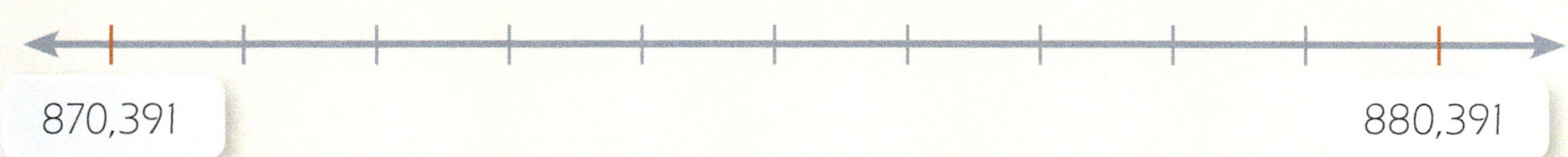

Which is the smallest number? ▶ ______

Exam Strategies

Multiple-Choice Questions

1. Which number is missing on the number line?

A. 200,000

B. 270,000

C. 300,000

D. 320,000

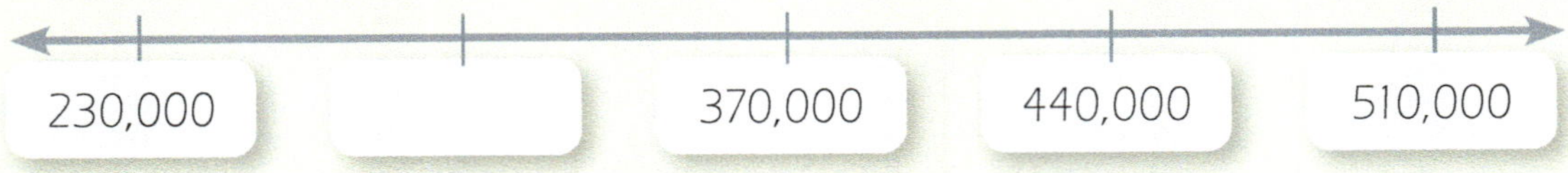

Analyzing the Answers

A. 200,000 would be on the left on the number line of all the numbers shown because it's 30,000 less than 230,000.

B. 270,000 would be located between 230,000 and 370,000. But the interval of the number line is 70,000 and 270,000 is 40,000 greater than 230,000 and 100,000 less than 370,000.

C. 300,000 would be located between 230,000 and 370,000 and the interval between the numbers is 70,000. 300,00 is 70,000 greater than 230,00 and 70,000 is less than 370,000.

D. 320,000 would be located between 230,000 and 370,000. But the interval of the number line is 70,000 and 320,000 is 90,000 greater than 230,000 and 50,000 less than 370,000.

▸ Therefore, the correct answer is **C**.

1. A B C D

What Did You Learn?

Final Evaluation

1. Match each number with its word form.

points
/ 3

a. 465,308

b. 700,294

c. 198,610

- one hundred ninety-eight thousand, six hundred one
- four hundred sixty-five thousand, three hundred eight
- one hundred ninety-eight thousand, six hundred ten
- seven hundred, two hundred ninety-four
- four hundred seventy-five thousand, three hundred eight
- seven hundred thousand, two hundred ninety-four

2. Complete by composing or decomposing the numbers.

points
/ 4

a. 678,038

_______ **HTh** + _______ **TTh** + _______ **Th** + _______ **H** + _______ **T** + _______ **O**

b. 910,674

900,000 + _________ + _________ + _________ + _________

c. 700,000 + 50,000 + 8,000 + 300 + 40 + 2

[ ]

d. 3 **HTh** + 4 **TTh** + 5 **Th** + 2 **H** + 2 **T** + 1 **O**

[ ]

3. Color the numbers greater than 600,000 in yellow and those less than 500,000 in blue.

points /4

a.

HTh	TTh	Th	H	T	O
6	0	4	5	9	2

c.

HTh	TTh	Th	H	T	O
8	9	4	9	8	2

b.

HTh	TTh	Th	H	T	O
4	9	3	3	1	6

d.

HTh	TTh	Th	H	T	O
3	7	1	8	3	5

4. Write >, < or =.

points /6

a. 734,495 ◯ 923,650

b. 195,384 ◯ 159,845

c. 946,318 ◯ 786,365

d. 231,954 ◯ 301,739

e. 606,385 ◯ 400,673

f. 304,586 ◯ 304,586

5. Mark the intervals on the number line and place the numbers in order. Then answer.

points /3

a. 100,500 102,500 102,000 101,000 101,500

Which number is the greatest? ▶ ______

Which number is the smallest? ▶ ______

Mark the correct answer with an ✕.

points

/ 4

6. The number "seven hundred eighty-one thousand, three hundred twelve" is written as:

A. 681,312

B. 781,320

C. 781,312

D. 718,312

7. The number 493,503 is written as:

A. Four hundred ninety-three thousand, five hundred thirty

B. Four hundred ninety-three thousand, five hundred three

C. Four hundred three thousand, five hundred three

D. Four hundred thirty-nine thousand, five hundred three

8. The place value of the highlighted digit in the number 864,387 is:

A. 600,000

B. 60,000

C. 6,000

D. 600

9. The decomposition of the number 583,479 is:

A. 500,000 + 3,000 + 400 + 70 + 9

B. 5 **HTh** + 8 **TTh** + 3 **Th** + 7 **H** + 4 **T** + 9 **O**

C. 500,000 + 80,000 + 3,000 + 400 + 70 + 9

D. 5 **HTh** + 3 **Th** + 4 **H** + 7 **T** + 9 **O**

points

/ 4

10. Which of the following numbers is **greater than** 396,538?

A. 269,853

B. 358,698

C. 358,963

D. 639,538

11. Which number is five hundred one thousand, two hundred three?

A. 501,203

B. 510,203

C. 501,230

D. 510,230

12. How many hundred thousands does 300,000 need to make one million?

A. 8 **HTh**

B. 7 **HTh**

C. 6 **HTh**

D. 5 **HTh**

13. In which position is the highlighted digit in 374,263?

A. Hundreds

B. Thousands

C. Ten Thousands

D. Hundred Thousands

Look at the number line and answer **questions 14–16**.

points

/ 3

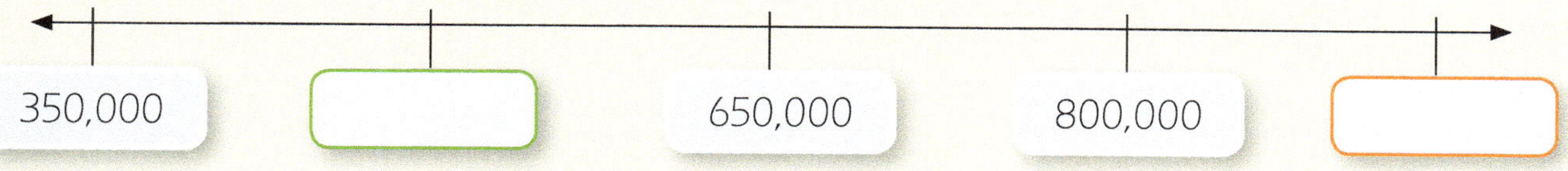

14. Which number goes in the ____ ?

A. 550,000

B. 400,000

C. 500,000

D. 450,000

---

15. Which number goes in the ____ ?

A. 850,000

B. 950,000

C. 890,000

D. 900,000

---

16. Which is the **smallest** number on the number line?

A. 650,000

B. 800,000

C. 550,000

D. 350,000

Find Test 3 Study Page

Unit 4

Fractions and Angles

In this unit you will learn to:

- read, write and represent fractions.
- compare and put fractions in order.
- solve addition and subtraction operations with fractions.
- measure and make angles using a protractor and compare them.
- understand the concept of symmetry.
- be positive and confident in yourself and your math skills.

Key Words

fraction

part-whole

mixed number

whole number

angle

line of symmetry

What Do You Know? Initial Evaluation

Look at the image and answer the questions.

1. What does the woman mean when she says "a quarter of a kilogram of cheese"?

2. What is the reference unit for the cheese?

3. Represent the woman's request as a fraction.

4. How many eggs are in half a carton?

5. What is the reference unit of the eggs?

Section 1

Fractions

The Concept of Part-Whole

Connecting

- How many tickets can the strand be divided into? ▶ ______ tickets.
- How many tickets will Rex get? ▶ ______ tickets.
- How would you represent three-fifths of the tickets? Color.

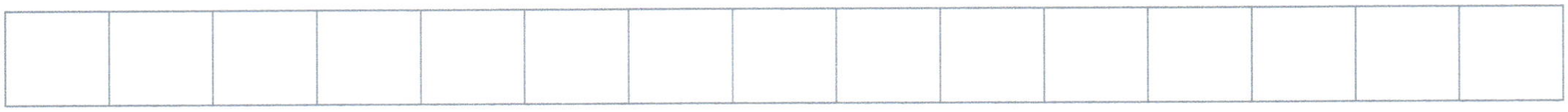

- How many tickets will Archie get? ▶ ______ tickets.

Learning

A fraction has a **numerator** and a **denominator**. The denominator is the number of **parts** we divide the **whole** into. The numerator is the number of parts we consider from the whole.

Example:

A cake is cut into 8 equal parts, and Karen eats 2 pieces.

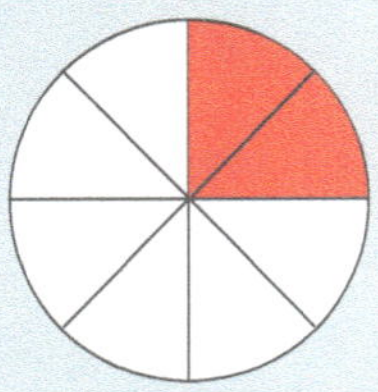

$\frac{2}{8}$ → 2 numerator, 8 denominator

The **whole** is the cake.

It has been cut into **8 equal parts**.

Karen ate 2 pieces; therefore, she ate $\frac{2}{8}$ of the cake.

Practicing

1. Identify the whole and the parts in each situation. Identify

a. Andrea cut a ribbon into two equal parts to make two bracelets.

Whole ▶ ____________________

Parts ▶ ____________________

b. In a class, six equal groups were formed.

Whole ▶ ____________________

Parts ▶ ____________________

2. Write the fraction that is represented in each case. Represent

a. 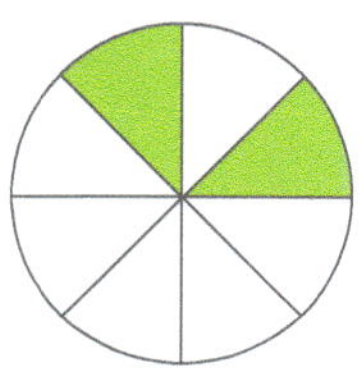 $\frac{\square}{\square}$

c. 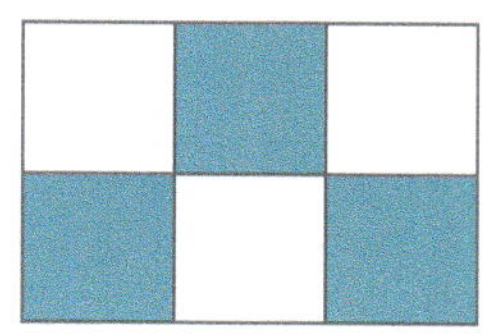 $\frac{\square}{\square}$

b. 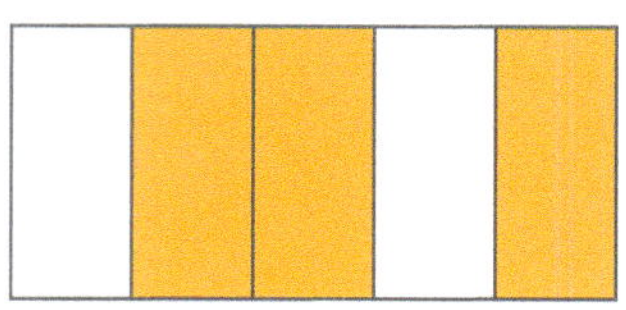 $\frac{\square}{\square}$

d. 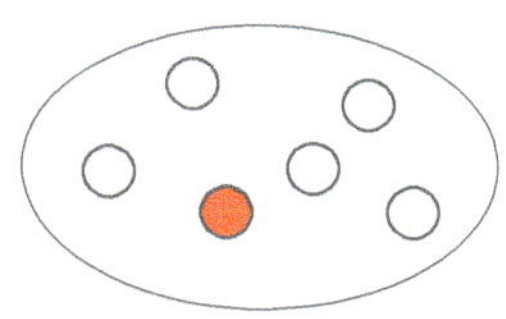 $\frac{\square}{\square}$

3. Write the fraction described in each situation. Apply

a. In a box with 12 colored pencils, 2 are red.

The fraction that represents the red pencils is $\frac{\square}{\square}$.

b. At a birthday party, a cake was cut into 12 equal parts and 3 pieces were left over.

The fraction that represents the pieces of cake that were left over is $\frac{\square}{\square}$.

c. In a box with 20 apples, 12 are green and 8 are red.

The fraction that represents the green apples is $\frac{\square}{\square}$.

Reading and Writing Fractions

Connecting

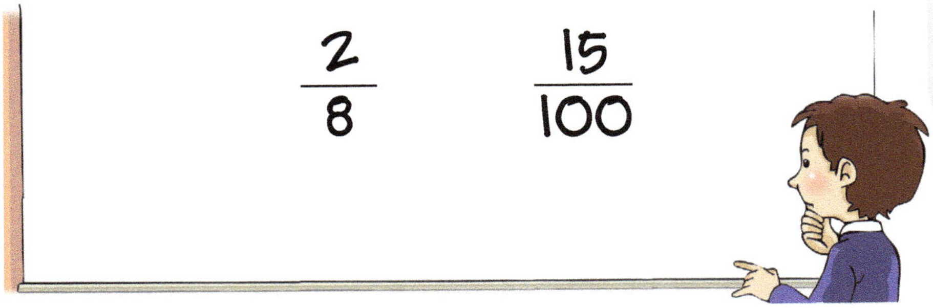

- When we read a fraction, do we say the numerator or the denominator first?

____

- What is the answer to the boy's question? Explain.

____

____

- The numerator in a fraction is read according to the number it represents. Does the same thing happen with the denominator? Give an example.

____

____

Learning

To **read** and **write fractions** you say the number in the numerator. Then the denominator is expressed as follows:

2 is read as **half**.
3 is read as **third**.
4 is read as **fourth** or **quarter**.
5 is read as **fifth**.
6 is read as **sixth**.
7 is read as **seventh**.
8 is read as **eighth**.
9 is read as **ninth**.
10 is read as **tenth**.
100 is read as **hundredth**.

Examples:

$\frac{4}{7}$ is read as four-sevenths.

$\frac{20}{100}$ is read as twenty-hundredths.

Practicing

1. Match each denominator. Understand

Denominator	Word Form
a. 5	fifths
b. 2	tenths
c. 10	halves

2. Write the following fractions in word form. Represent

a. $\frac{5}{6}$ ▶ ____________________

b. $\frac{12}{100}$ ▶ ____________________

c. $\frac{1}{10}$ ▶ ____________________

d. $\frac{3}{4}$ ▶ ____________________

e. $\frac{5}{8}$ ▶ ____________________

3. Read the word problem and circle the fractions that appear in it. Relate

Ms. Green is cooking some rice. First, she puts a tablespoon of oil and three-fourths of a cup of rice into a pot. She stirs it and adds one-half of a cube of vegetable stock and five-sixths of a teaspoon of salt. She finally adds two cups of water and waits for the water to evaporate.

turn from liquid to vapor

$\frac{5}{5}$ $\frac{1}{3}$ $\frac{5}{7}$ $\frac{3}{4}$ $\frac{4}{3}$ $\frac{5}{6}$ $\frac{1}{2}$

Representing Fractions

Connecting

bread

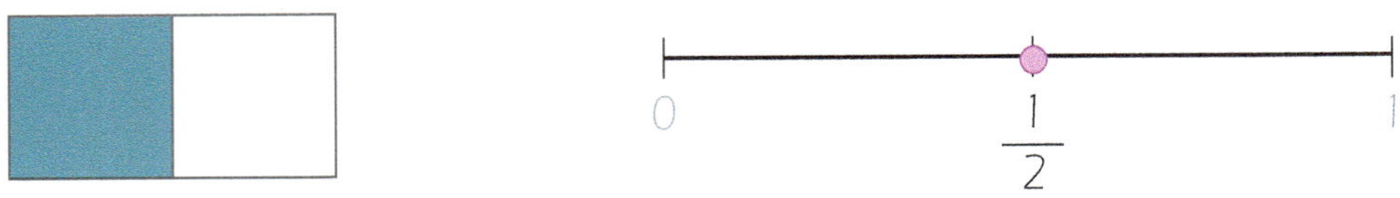

yogurt

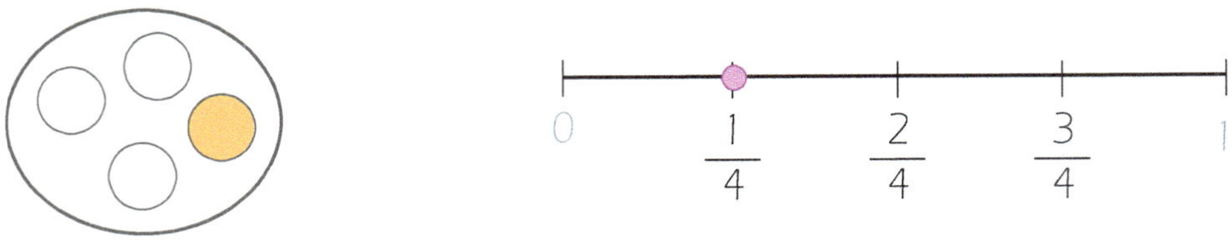

- In how many ways was the bread that Daniel ate represented?

____

- How many parts was the number line divided into between 0 and 1? ▶ Into ☐ parts.
- In how many ways was the yogurt that Daniel ate represented?

____

- How many parts was the number line divided into between 0 and 1? ▶ Into ☐ parts.
- How many ways can a fraction be represented?

____

Education through Values

Eating balanced meals gives you energy, helps you grow stronger and keeps you healthy.

Learning

A fraction can be represented in sections, with sets and on number lines.

Example: Represent $\frac{5}{6}$.

- **Section:**
  The figure is divided into equals parts according to the denominator, and the parts are colored as indicated by the numerator.

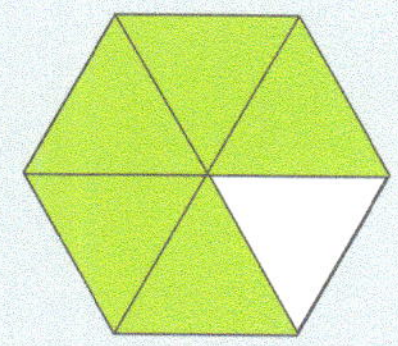

- **Set:**
  An amount of elements is divided into subgroups with the same amount of elements according to the denominator. The colored ones represent the numerator.

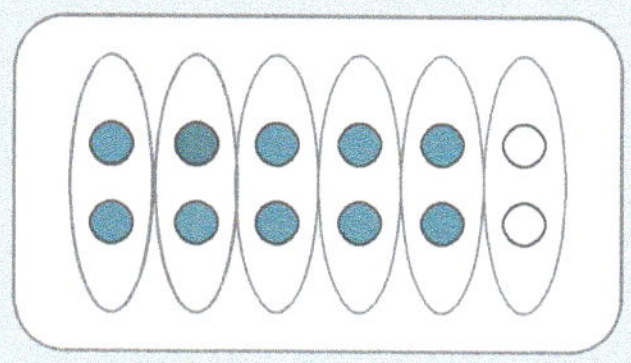

- **Number Line:**
  Divide the number line between two whole numbers. Divide it into equal intervals indicated by the denominator. Then locate the fraction that is represented.

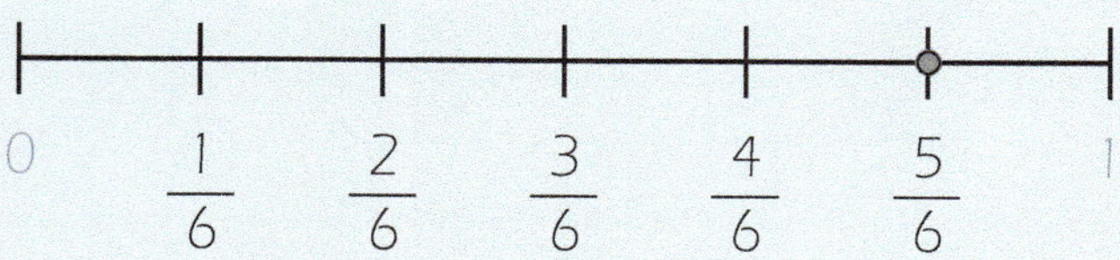

Practicing

1. Write the fraction that is represented in each case. Represent

a.

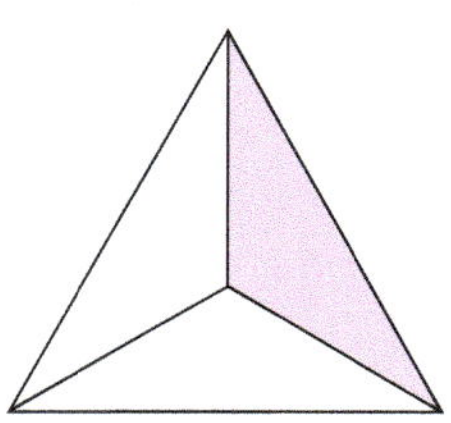

b.

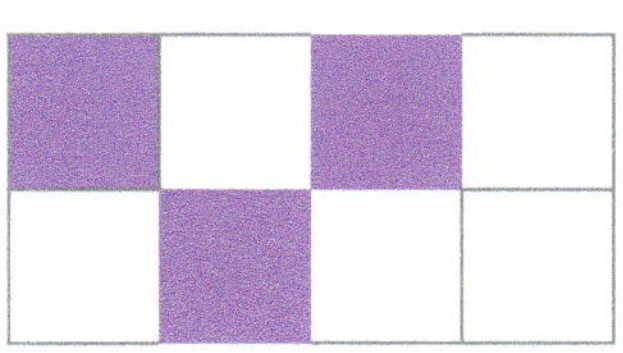

c.

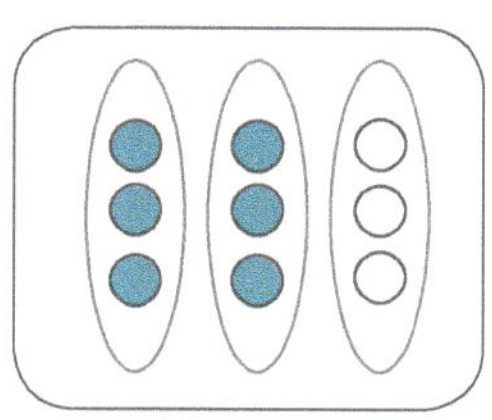

d.

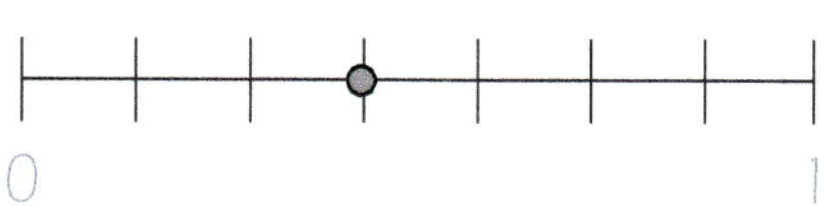

2. Represent each fraction in a **section**. Represent

a. $\frac{4}{5}$

b. $\frac{2}{3}$

c. $\frac{1}{8}$

d. $\frac{4}{6}$

3. Represent each fraction with a **set**. Represent

a group or collection of something

a. $\frac{1}{6}$

b. $\frac{3}{5}$

c. $\frac{5}{8}$

d. $\frac{3}{10}$

4. Represent each fraction on a **number line**. Represent

a. $\frac{3}{4}$

0 1

b. $\frac{7}{10}$

0 1

5. Write the fraction described in every situation and represent it. Apply

a. There are eight teams in a competition. Three of the teams are coed. What fraction of the teams are coed?

having boys and girls

Set

b. Kate has ten comic books, five of which are about superheroes. What fraction of the comic books are about superheroes?

Number Line

c. Patrick divided his sandwich into four equal parts and shared it with three friends. What fraction of the sandwich does each person have?

Section

6. Mark the representations of $\frac{9}{10}$ with a ✔. Analyze

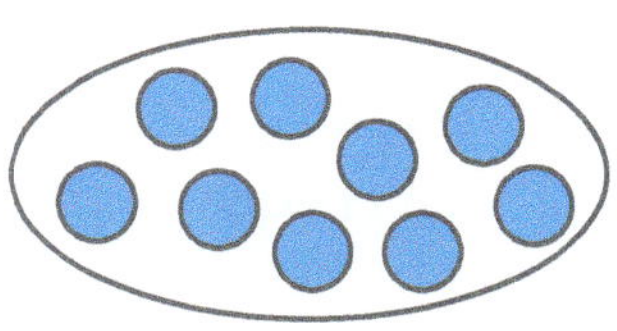

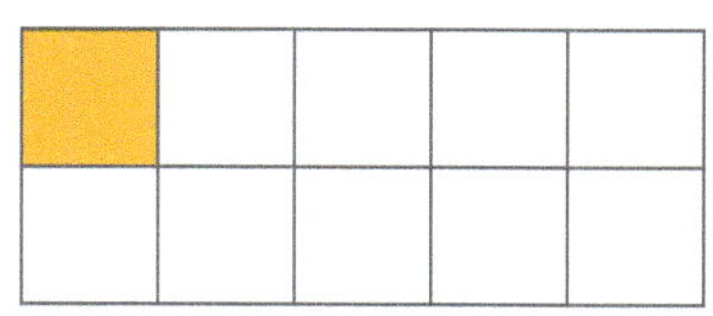

Mixed Numbers

Connecting

- Did the girl eat more or less than a plate? Why?

____

____

- What is the point of reference used in the situation?

____

Learning

A **mixed number** is a **whole number** and a **fraction**.

Example:

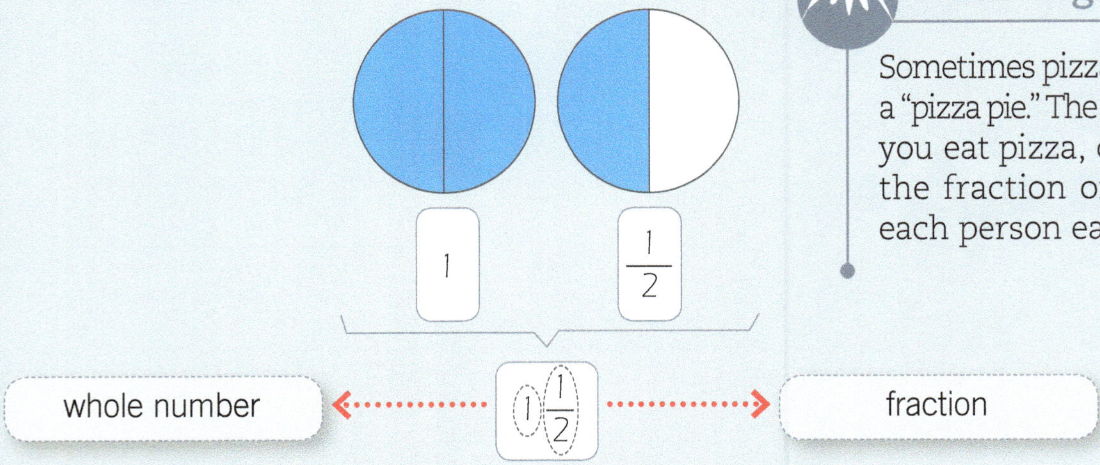

You read it as one and a half.

Challenge

Sometimes pizza is called a "pizza pie." The next time you eat pizza, calculate the fraction of the pie each person eats!

Practicing

1. In the following mixed numbers, circle the whole part in orange and the fraction in green. Understand

a.

b.

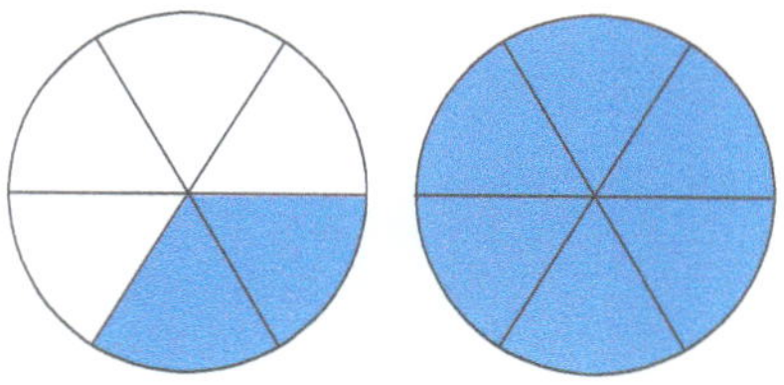

c.

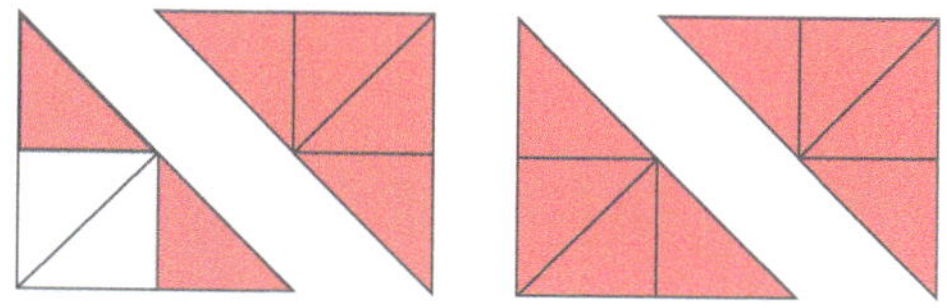

d.

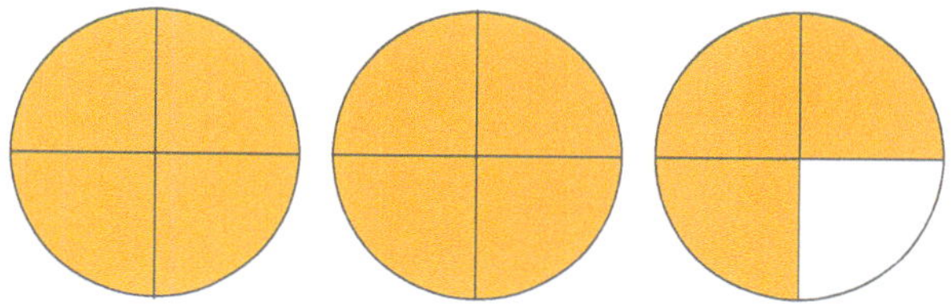

2. Write the mixed number. Represent

a.

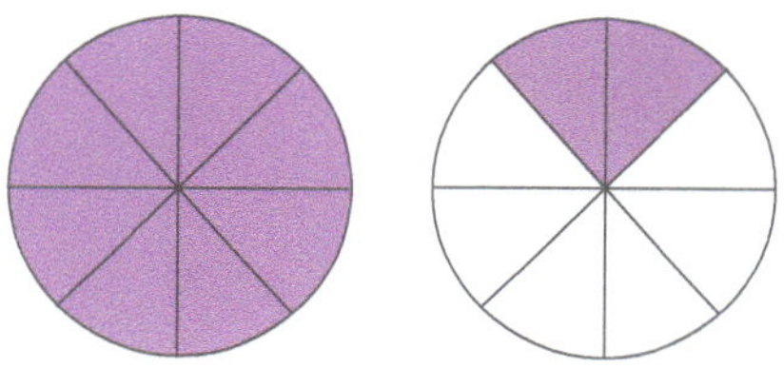

b.

c.

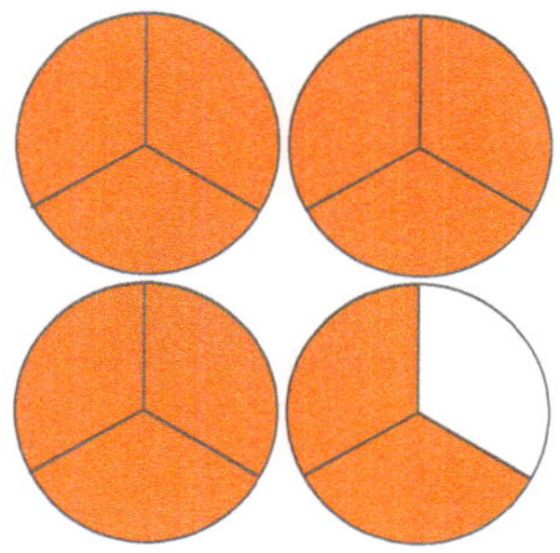

d.

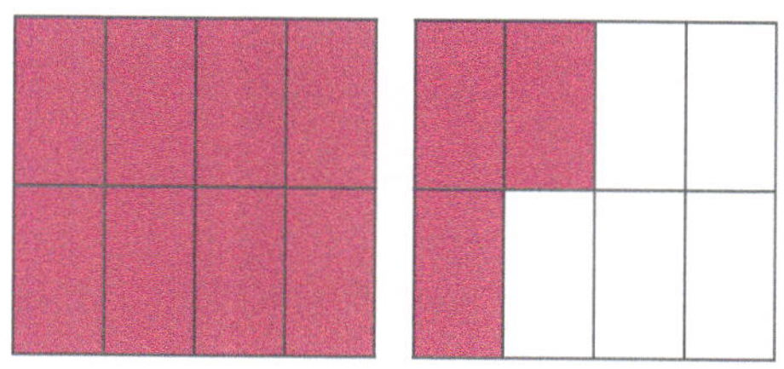

Quiz Yourself

Represent the following mixed numbers.

a. $2\frac{1}{6}$

b. $4\frac{2}{3}$

Measuring Angles with a Protractor

Connecting

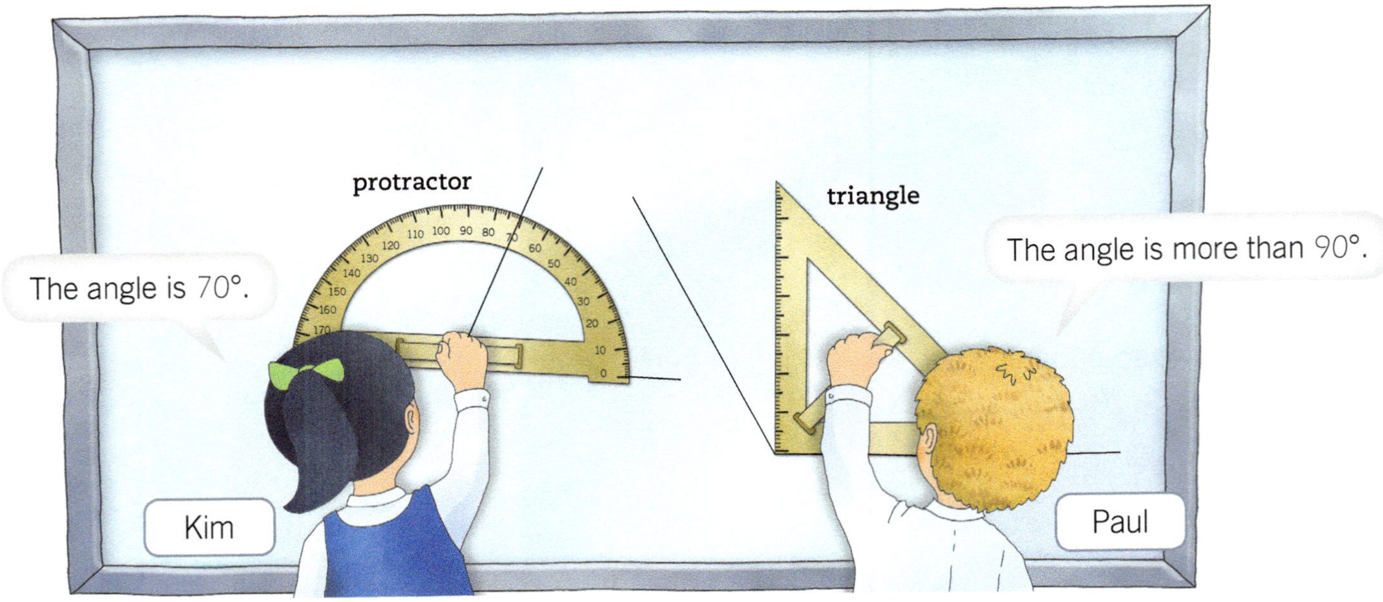

Did You Know...?

Angle comes from the Latin word "angulus" which means "a corner."

- Which instrument did each person use to measure the angles? Write them.

 ▶ ____________________ 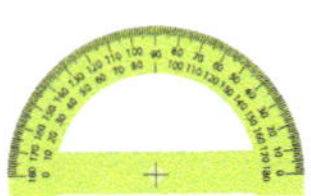 ▶ ____________________

- Why did Paul say that the angle is **more** than 90°? How does he know? Explain.

____

____

- Which instrument gives an exact measurement? Explain.

____

____

Learning

half of a circle

To **measure angles** you can use a **protractor**, which is a semicircle divided into 180 equal parts. These parts are called degrees (°). An angle is measured by the number of degrees it has.

To measure angles you should:

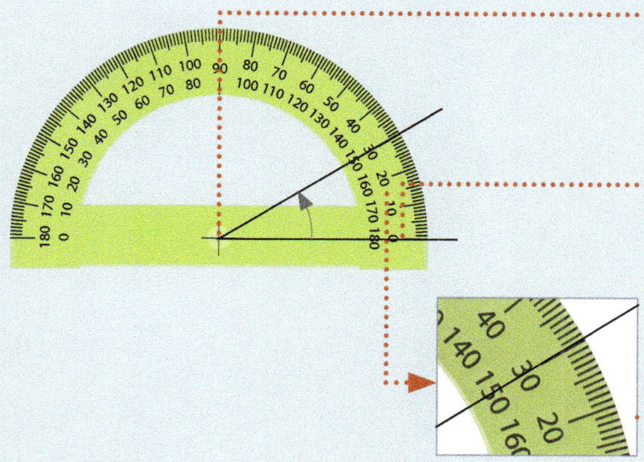

- Match the center of the protractor with the vertex of the angle.
- Align one side of the angle with 0° on the protractor. The angle is measured **counter-clockwise**.
- The number the other side marks on the protractor is its measurement.

In this case, the angle is 30°.

Practicing

1. Look at each angle and mark whether its measurement is greater or less than 90°. Recognize

a.

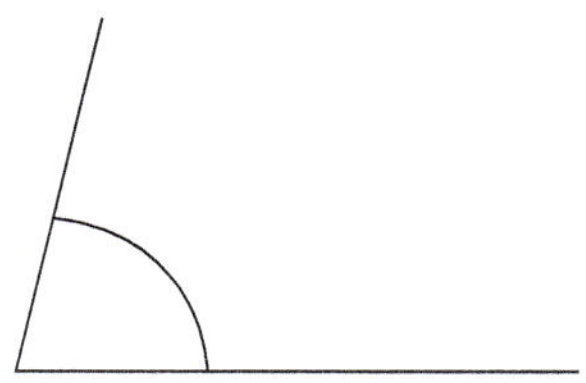

☐ greater than 90°

☐ less than 90°

b.

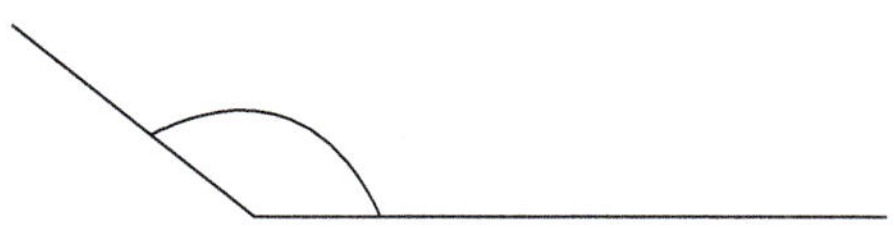

☐ greater than 90°

☐ less than 90°

c.

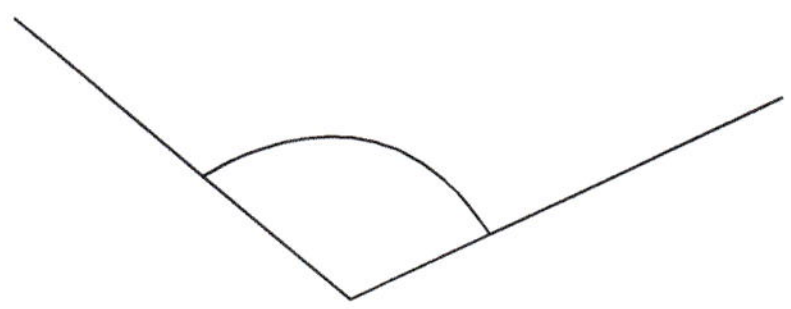

☐ greater than 90°

☐ less than 90°

d.

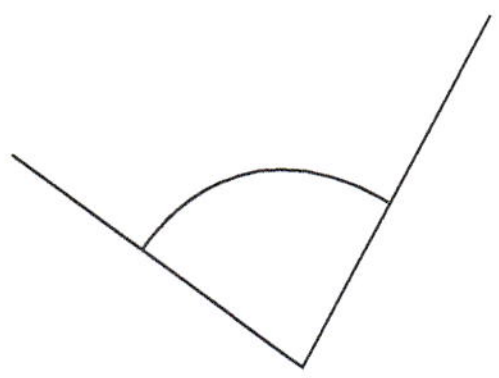

☐ greater than 90°

☐ less than 90°

2. Determine the measurement of each angle. Apply

a.

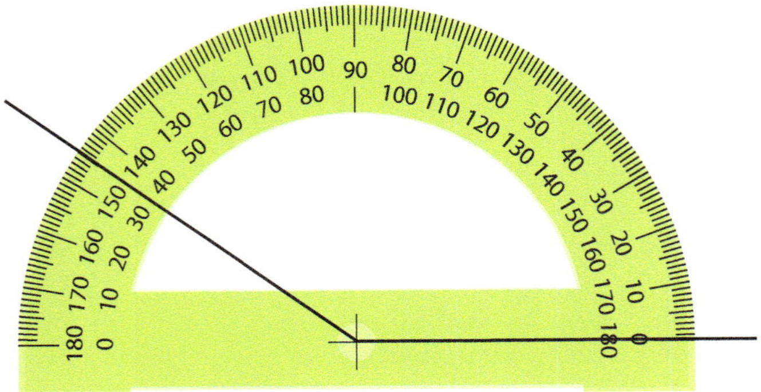

The angle is ______.

The measurement of an angle corresponds to the opening between its sides, not the length.

b.

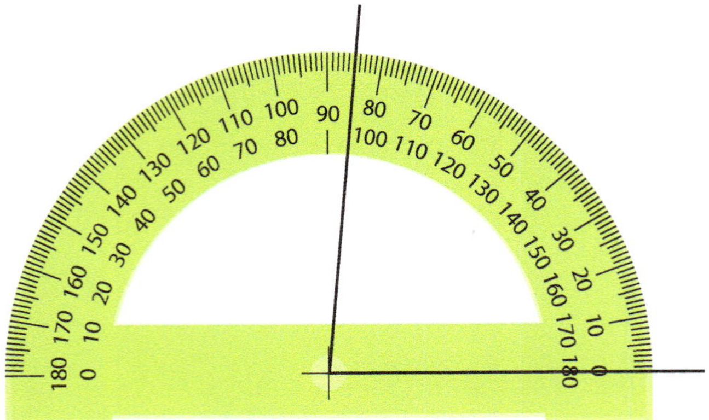

The angle is ______.

Challenge

Take a look around. Draw shapes and angles you see. Estimate the measurement of the angles. Share with your class.

c.

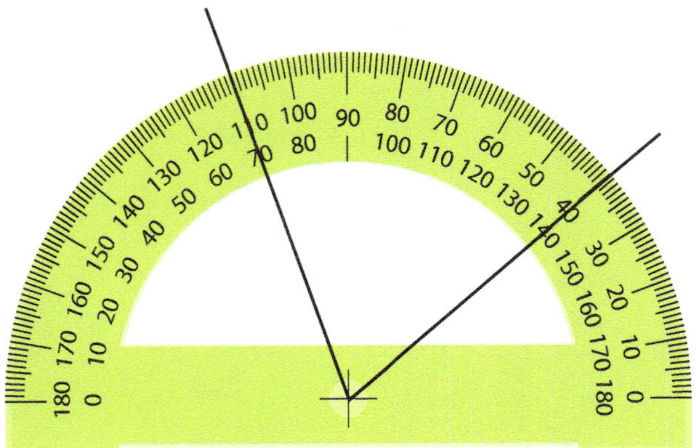

The angle is ______.

If the protractor is not correctly placed, can you still get an accurate measurement?

3. Use a protractor to measure the angles. Apply

a.

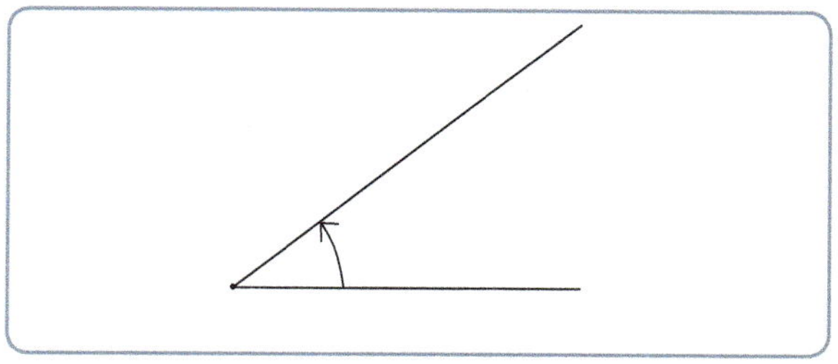

The angle is ☐.

d.

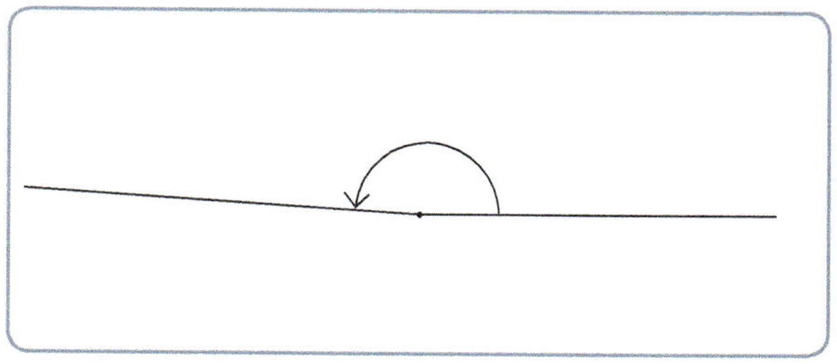

The angle is ☐.

b.

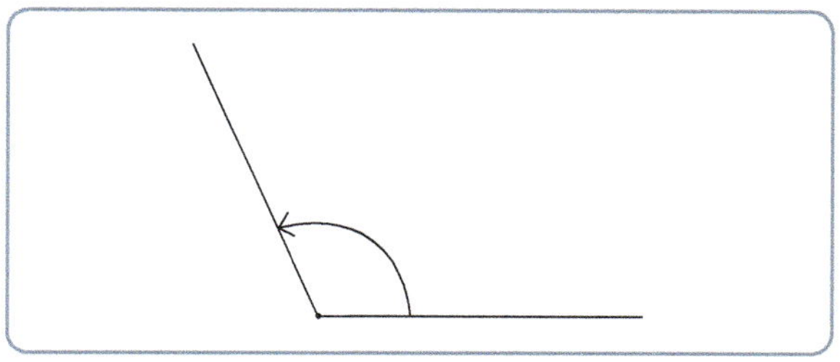

The angle is ☐.

e.

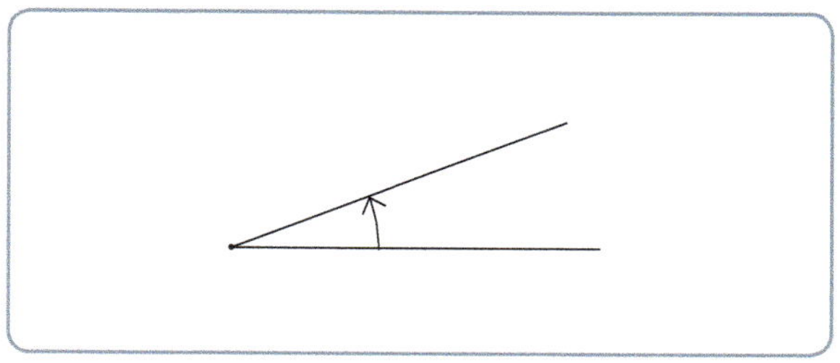

The angle is ☐.

c.

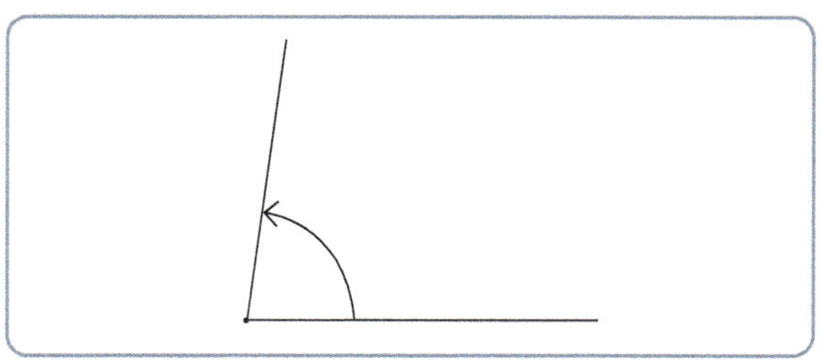

The angle is ☐.

f.

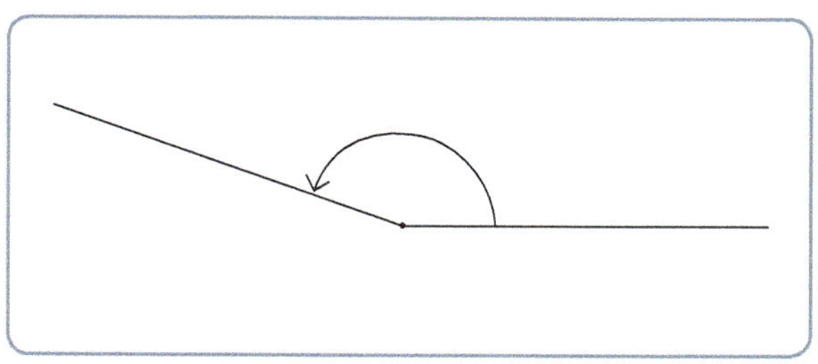

The angle is ☐.

Making Angles with a Protractor

Connecting

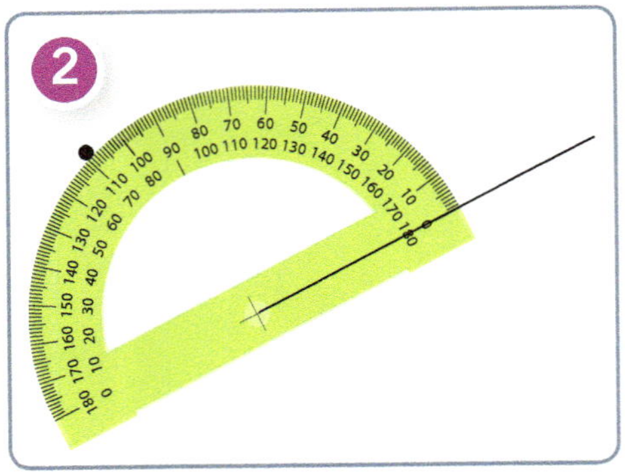

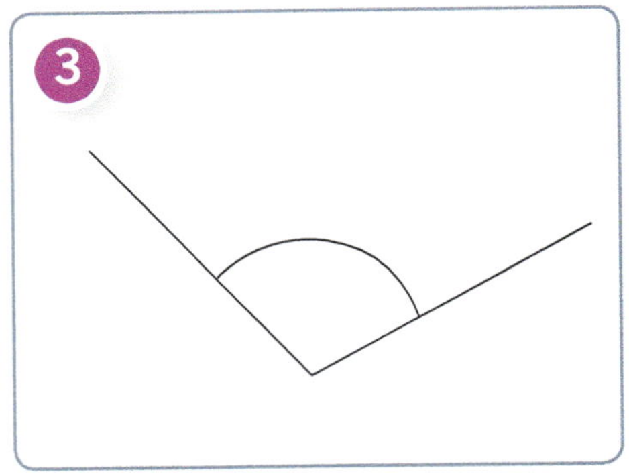

- What is shown in image 1? ▶ ______________________________
- How many degrees does the dot in image 2 represent? ▶ ______________________________
- What are the characteristics of the angle in image 3?

____

____

Learning

To make an angle using a protractor, follow these steps:

1st

Draw a **line segment**.

2nd

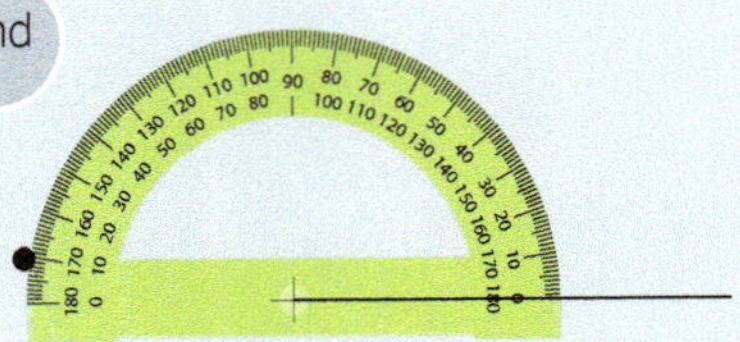

Place the protractor at the end of the line segment and align it with 0° on the protractor. Then mark the measurement of the angle you want with a dot. In this case, the measurement is 170°.

3rd

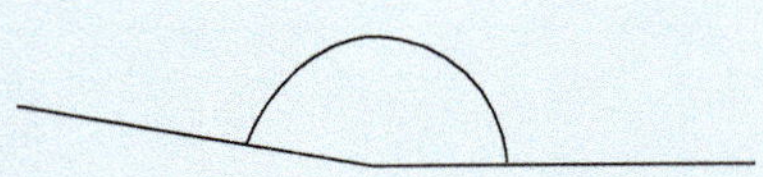

Using the protractor, mark the angle you want to make and join the vertex with the dot made.

Practicing

1. Make the angles asked for. Apply

a. A 38° angle.

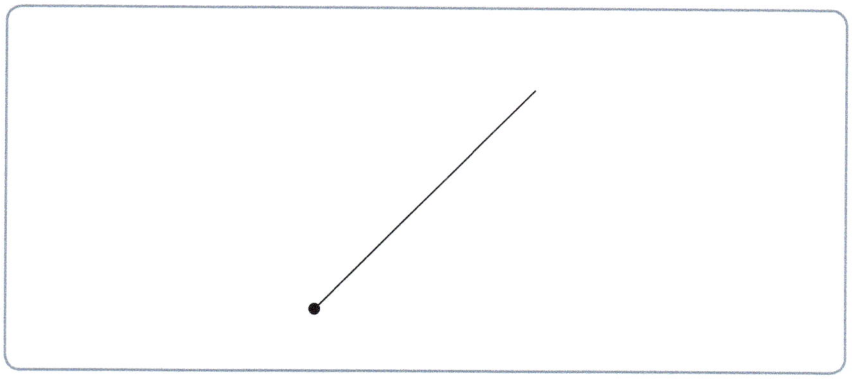

b. A 100° angle.

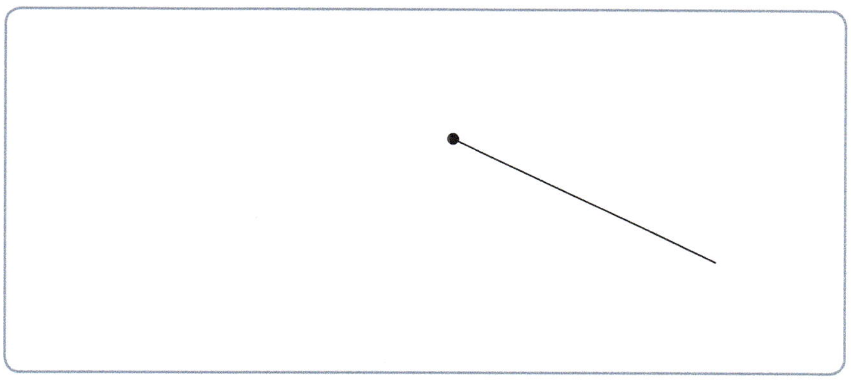

c. A 163° angle.

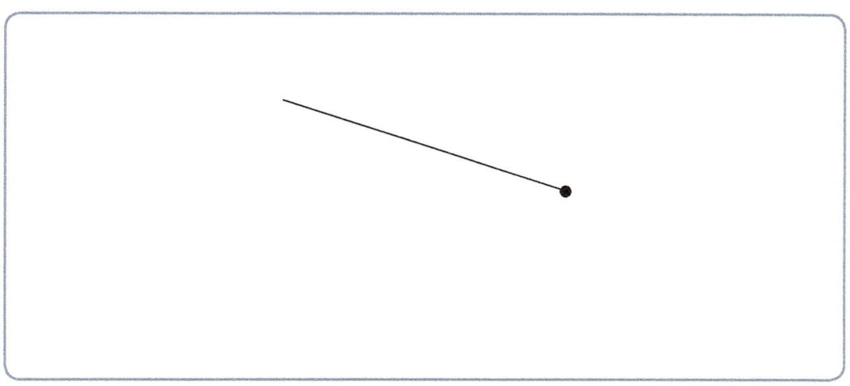

Tip

An angle that is opened to the right is measured counter-clockwise. If the angle is opened to the left, it is measured clockwise.

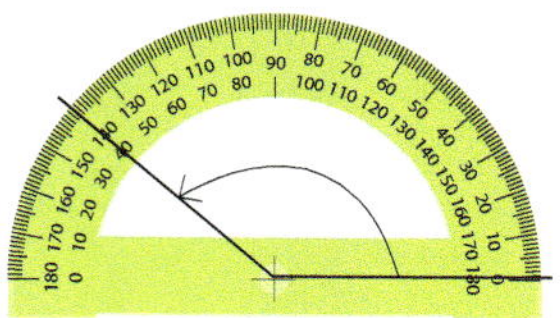

Education through Values

When we face difficult tasks, we can always count on our family and our classmates for help. Value working in teams!

Comparing Angles

Connecting

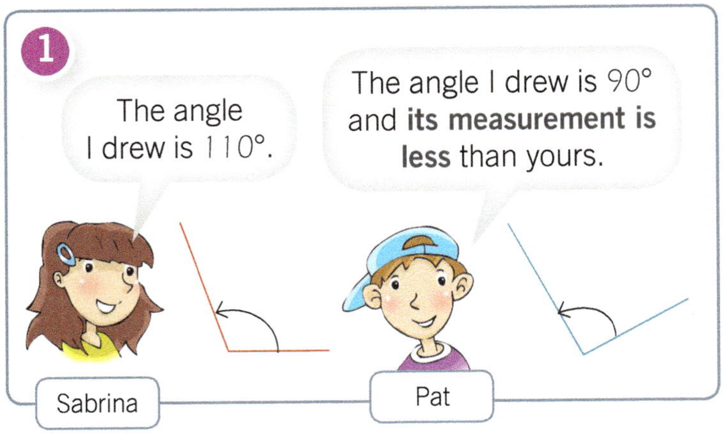

- How did Pat know that the measurement of his angle was less than Sabrina's? Explain.

- Look at image 2. What did Sabrina do to check that Pat's angle measurement was less than hers? Explain.

Learning

To **compare angles** you have to compare their measurements. The larger number will be the one with the greater angle.

You can also compare by putting the two angles on top of each other and checking their measurements.

Example:

A 60° angle is **greater than** a 30° angle.

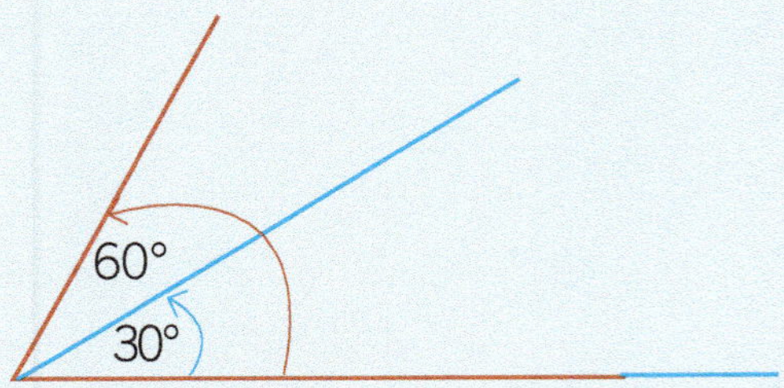

Practicing

1. Compare the measurements of each pair of angles and complete with **greater than** or **less than**. Then draw the angles to check your answers. Analyze

a. A 97° angle is ______________________ a 107° angle.

b. A 140° angle is ______________________ a 135° angle.

Quiz Yourself

Read the situation and answer.

What time is it if the hands of the clock make a 90° angle? Is there only one possibility? Explain.

Lines of Symmetry

Connecting

1
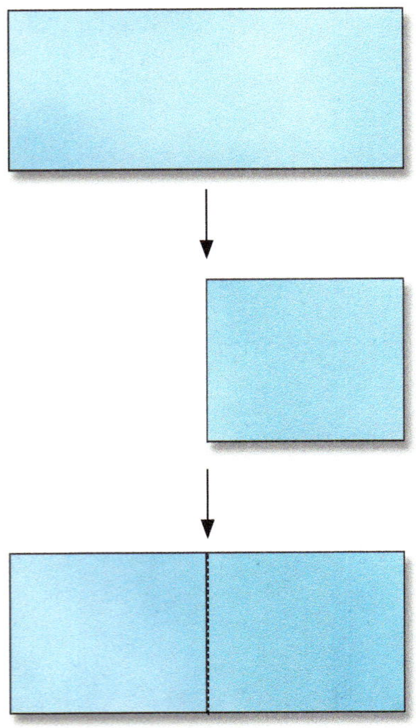

2
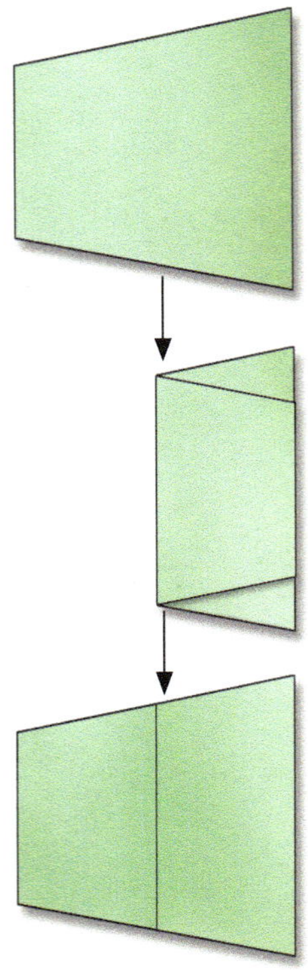

- Describe what was done to the figures.

- When folding the figures in half and unfolding them, what are the resulting figures? Compare them.

Learning

A **line of symmetry** is a line that divides a figure into two equal parts of the same shape and size. A figure does not always have a line of symmetry, but some have one or more.

Example:

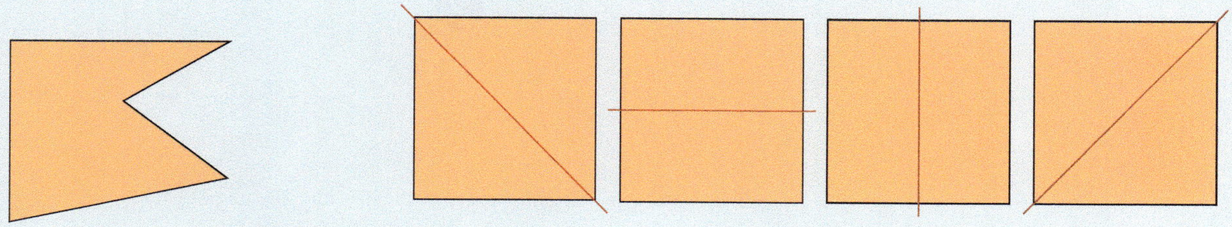

Figure **with no** line of symmetry.

Figure with **multiple** lines of symmetry.

Practicing

1. Using **Cutout 1** on **page 159**, check if the line of symmetry is correct by folding the figure. Mark with a ✔ if it is correct. Check

a.

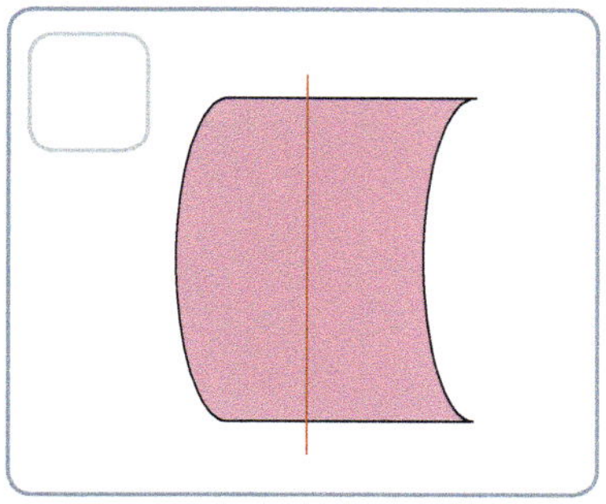

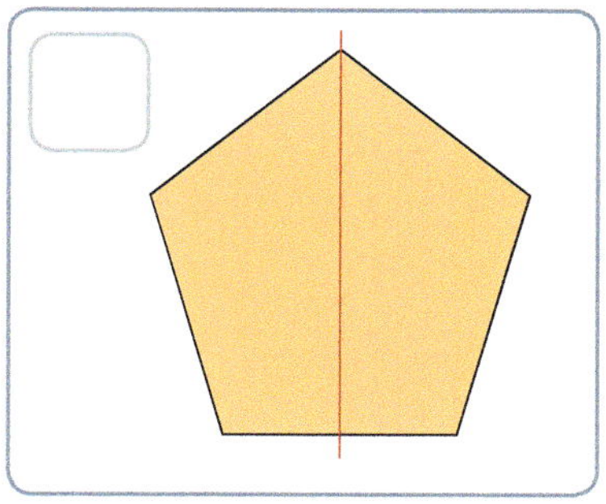

2. Draw a line of symmetry in each figure. Then answer. Apply

a.

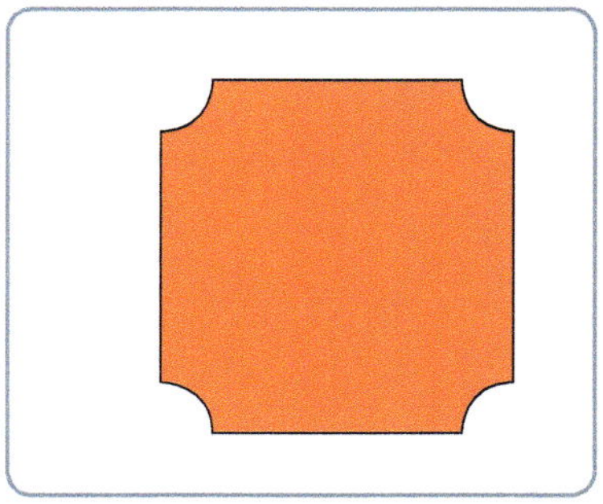

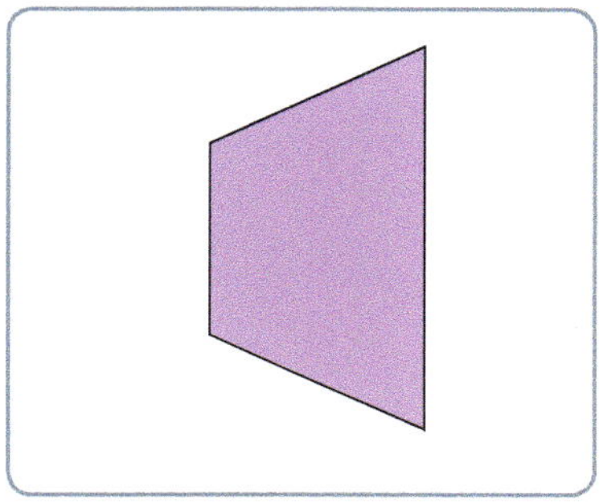

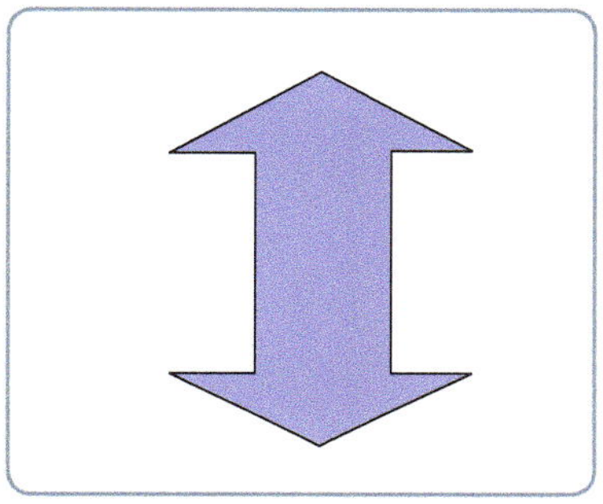

b. Compare your line of symmetry with those of your classmates. Are they the same? Can there be more than one line of symmetry for the figures? Discuss.

Identifying and Making Symmetrical Figures

Connecting

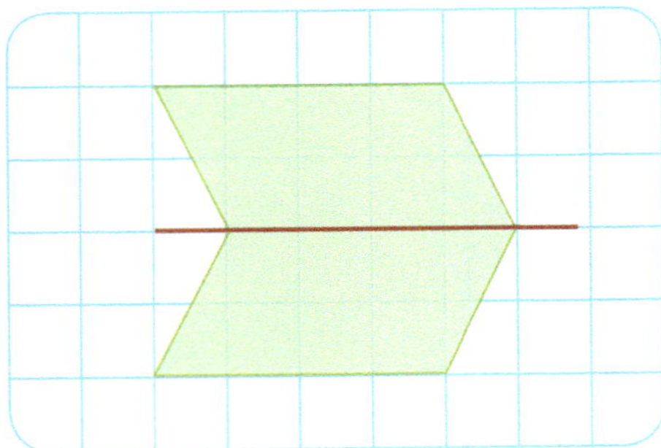

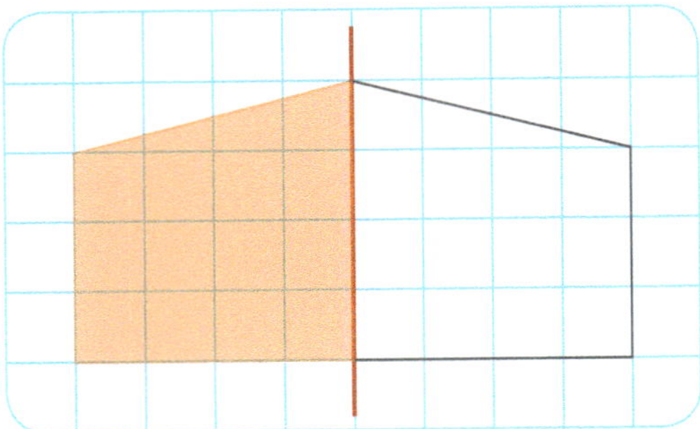

- Look at the line across figure 1. What can you conclude about this figure?

____

____

- What action is occurring in figure 2? Explain.

____

____

Learning

To **identify symmetric figures** you need to use a line of symmetry. If you want to **make symmetrical figures**, draw a line of symmetry and draw the same shape on both sides of it. This means that each figure will have the same distance and position in respect to the line of symmetry.

Example:

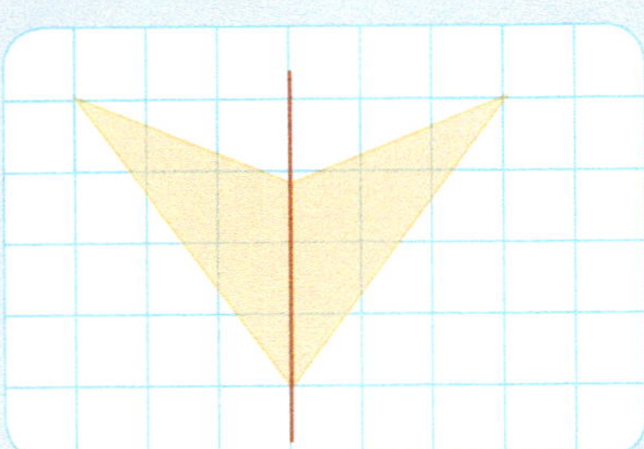

Symmetrical Figure

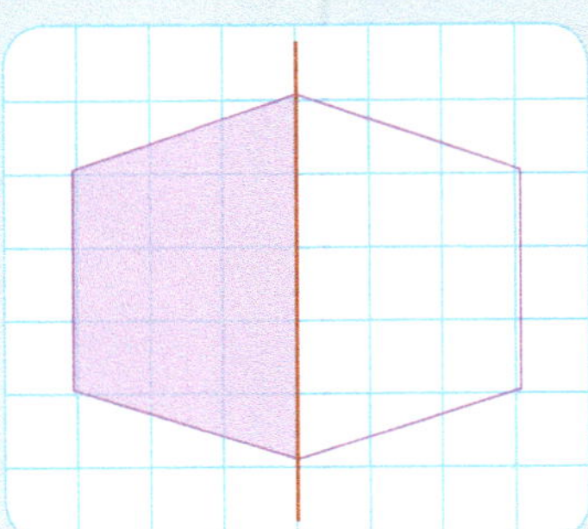

Making a Symmetrical Figure

Practicing

1. Circle the figures that are symmetric and draw a line of symmetry through them. Analyze

2. Complete the following symmetric figures. Apply

a.

b.

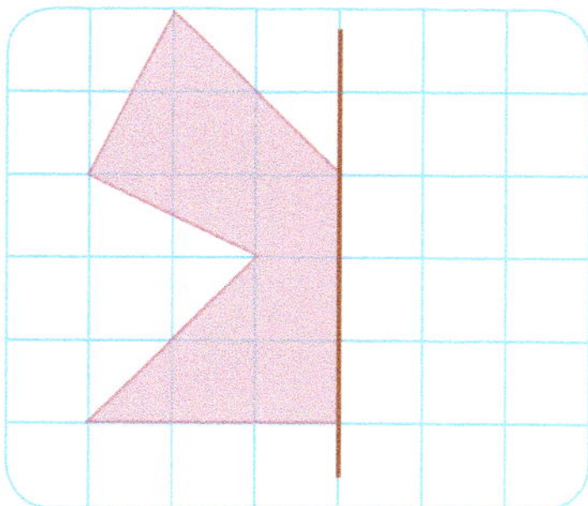

c.

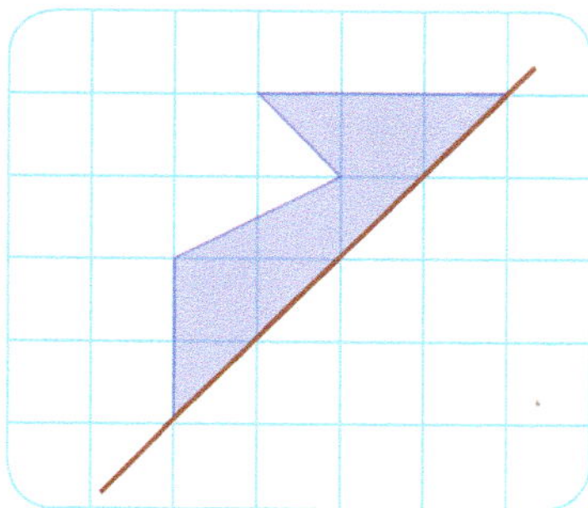

3. Starting from a line of symmetry, create a symmetric figure. Apply

a.

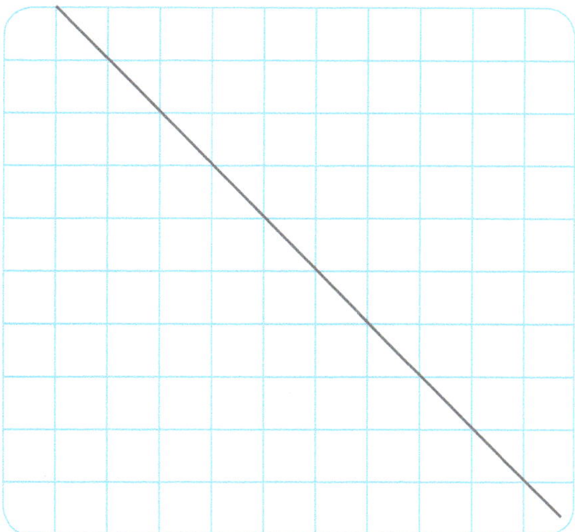

b.

Reflection: Axial Symmetry

Connecting

- What does reflection mean? Explain in your own words.

____

____

- Does a figure stay the same when you reflect it? Explain.

(Yes) (No), because ______________________________

____

- Do you think John and Peggy are correct? Explain.

____

____

Learning

One type of reflection is **axial** (relating to an axis) **symmetry**, where a figure is reflected based on an **axis** (line), called the **axis of reflection or symmetry**. All the points are the same distance from the axis in the original and the new figure, with the same size and shape on both sides.

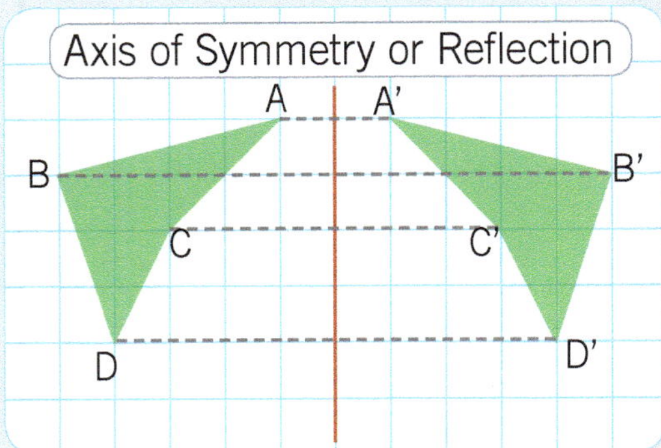

Practicing

1. Mark the figure with a (✔) that shows the axial symmetry of figure A. Identify

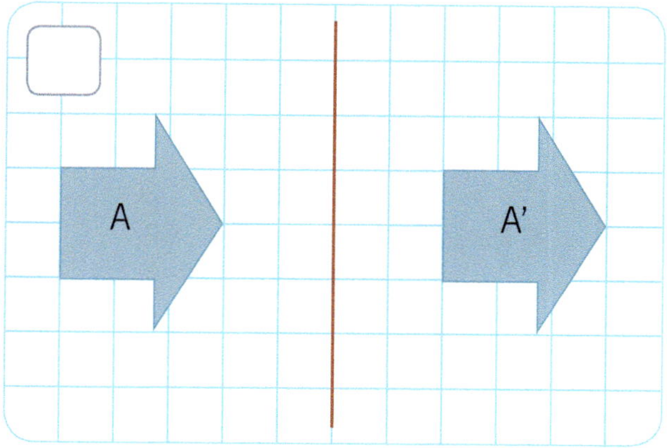

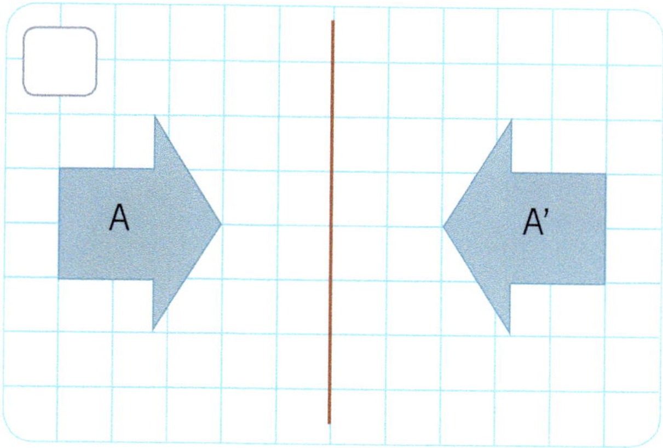

2. Reflect the figures using the line of symmetry or reflection. Apply

a.

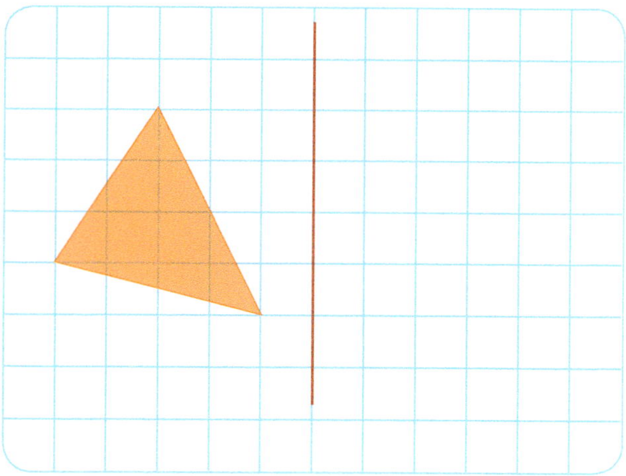

c.

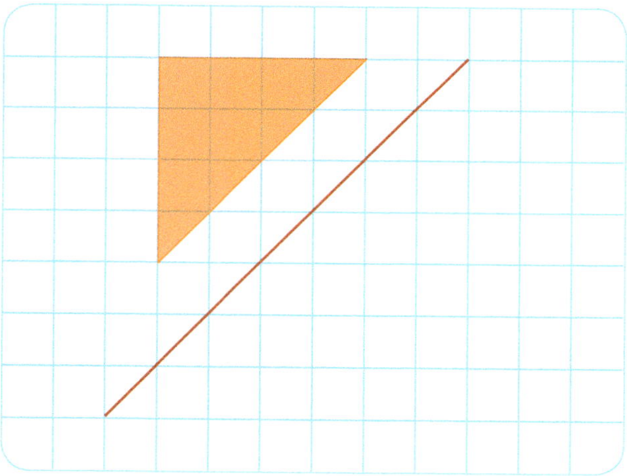

b.

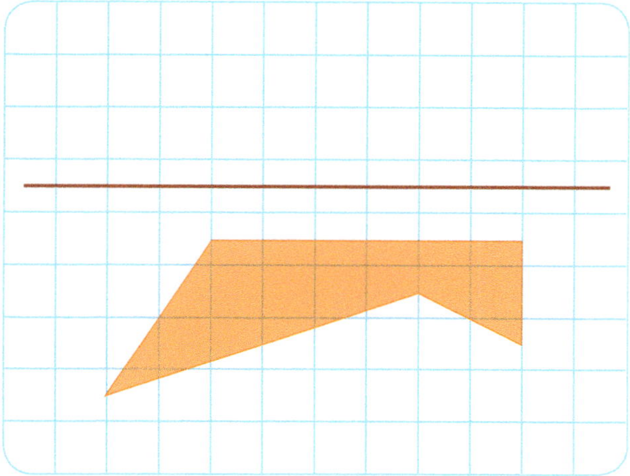

d.

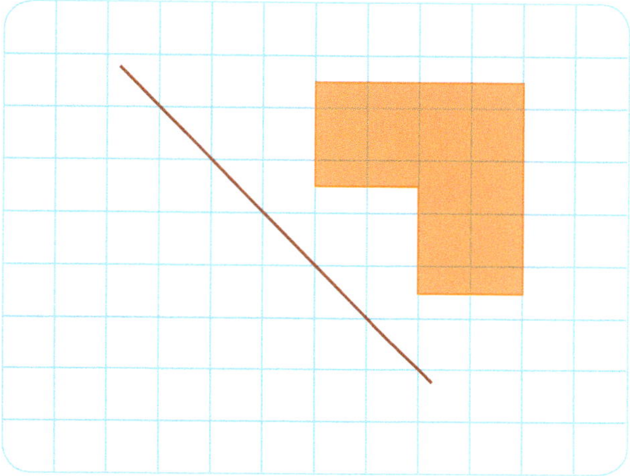

Let's Check!

The Concept of Part-Whole

1. Write the fraction represented in each case.

points ___ / 3

a.

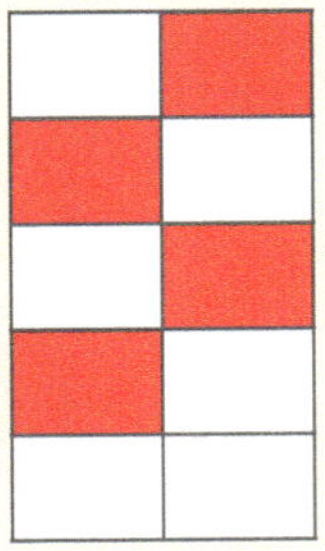

b.

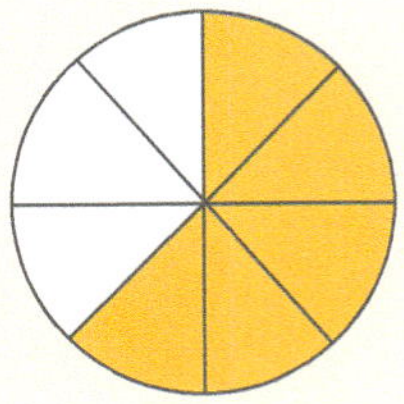

c.

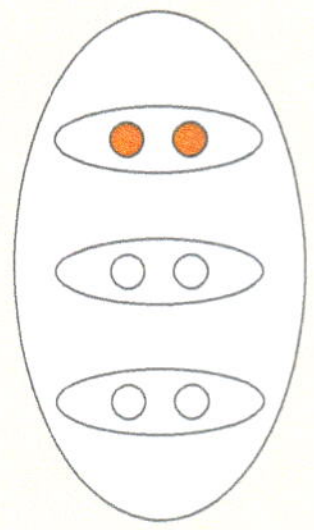

Reading and Writing Fractions

2. Match each fraction with its word form.

points ___ / 4

a.	$\frac{3}{8}$	five-tenths
b.	$\frac{3}{10}$	five-eighths
c.	$\frac{5}{8}$	three-tenths
d.	$\frac{5}{10}$	three-eighths

Representing Fractions

3. Represent the following fraction on the number line.

points ___ / 1

$\frac{3}{7}$

Mixed Numbers

4. Write the mixed numbers.

points
/ 2

a.

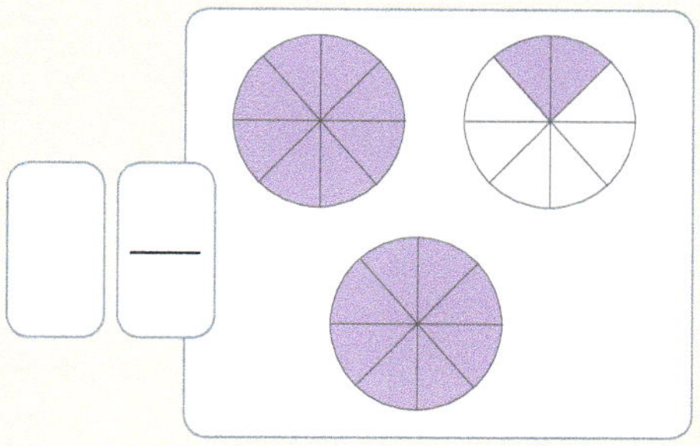

b.

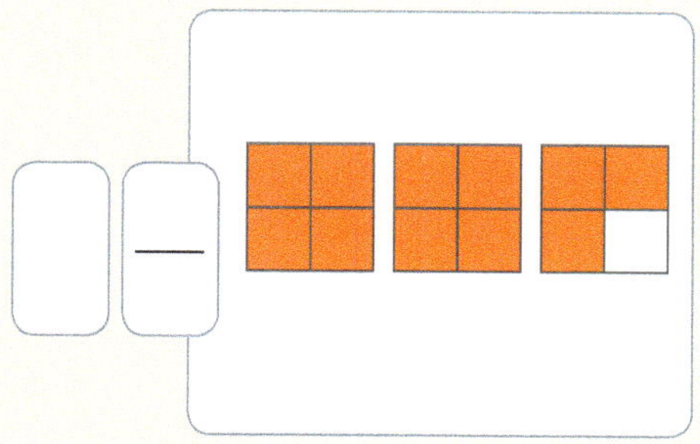

Measuring Angles

5. What is the measurement of the angle?

points
/ 1

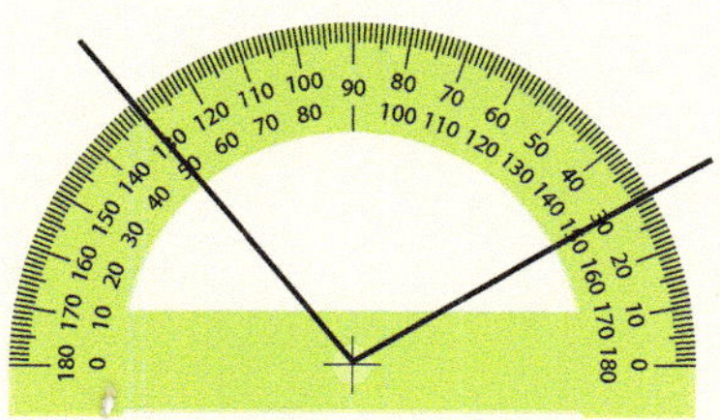

A. 100°

B. 120°

C. 130°

D. 150°

Comparing Angles

6. Which is true?

points
/ 1

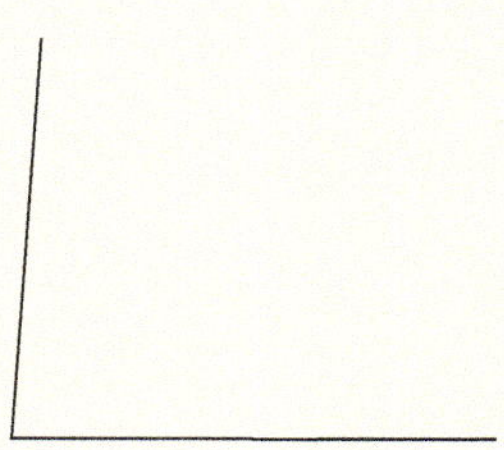

Angle 1

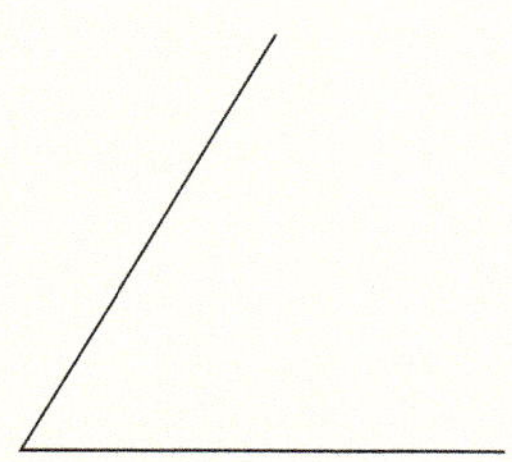

Angle 2

A. Angle 1 is greater than Angle 2.

B. Angle 1 and Angle 2 are equal.

C. Angle 1 is less than Angle 2.

D. Both angles are greater than 90°.

Exam Strategies

Multiple-Choice Questions

1. $\frac{1}{3}$ of the complete figure has been represented.

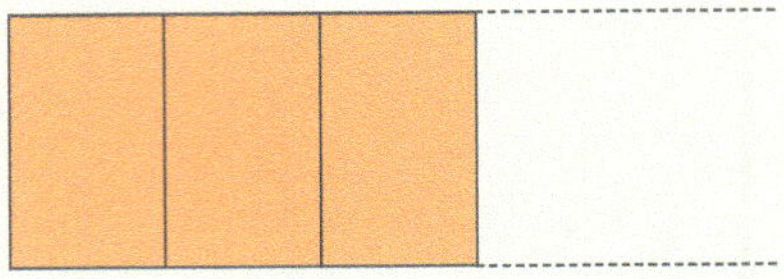

Which of the following representations corresponds to the complete figure?

A. 

B. 

C. 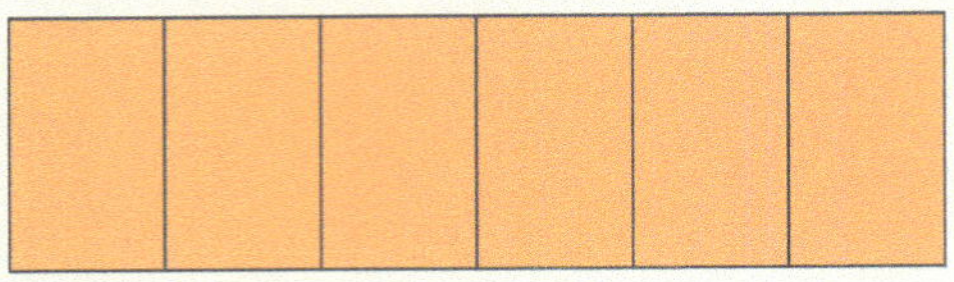

D. 

Analyzing the Answers

A. In this case, the representation shows 3 whole numbers divided into thirds.

B. In this case, the representation shows $\frac{3}{3}$, or the complete figure.

C. The representation here corresponds to $\frac{2}{3}$ of the complete figure.

D. In this case, the representation is $\frac{1}{3}$ of the figure.

▸ Therefore, the correct answer is **B**.

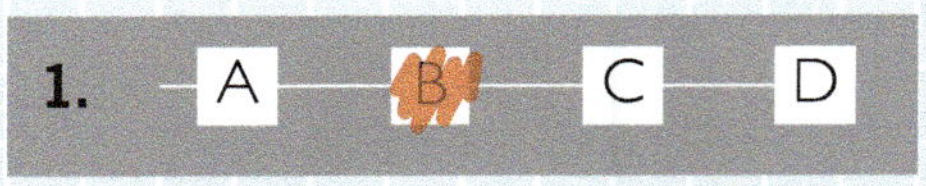

What Did You Learn?

Final Evaluation

1. Write the fraction represented in each case.

points
/ 4

a. 

b. 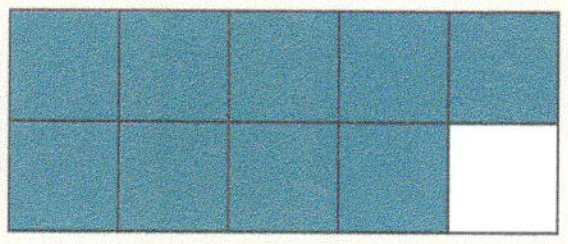

c. 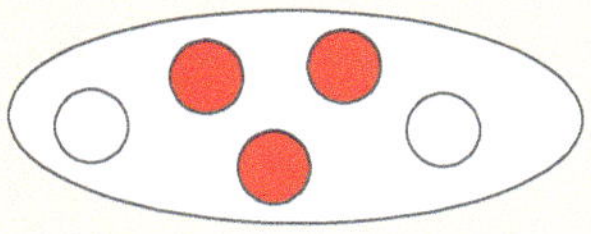

d. 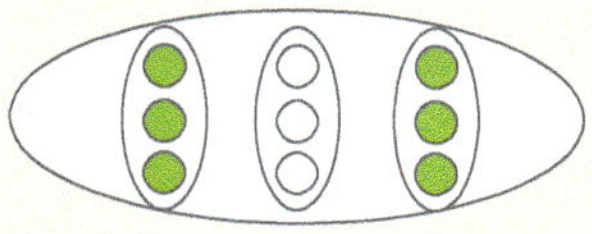

2. Match each fraction with its word form.

points
/ 4

a. $\frac{2}{8}$

b. $\frac{5}{7}$

c. $\frac{9}{10}$

d. $\frac{7}{8}$

- seven-eighths
- five-sevenths
- two-eighths
- seven-fifths
- eight-halves
- ten-ninths
- nine-tenths
- eight-sevenths

3. Represent the following fractions on the number lines.

points
/ 2

a. $\frac{3}{5}$ 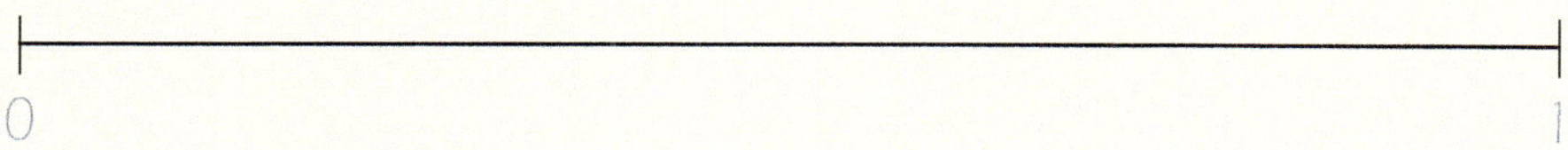

b. $\frac{2}{9}$ 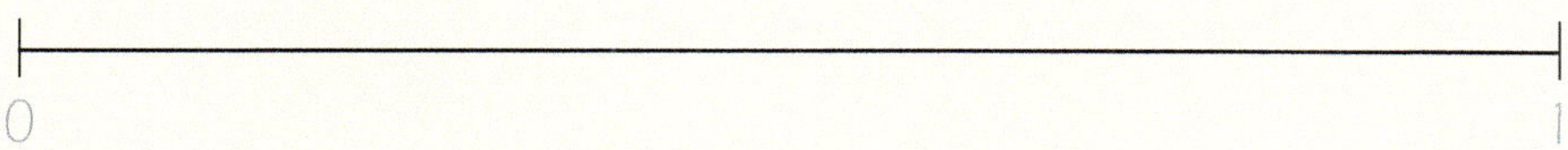

4. Represent each fraction.

points
/ 3

a. $\frac{3}{5}$ in a section.

b. $\frac{4}{7}$ with a set.

c. $\frac{3}{10}$ on a number line.

5. Choose and create a representation for the word problem.

points
/ 2

A construction company is building a 15-story building. If they have built $\frac{2}{3}$ of the building, how many more floors do they need to build?

- ☐ section
- ☐ set
- ☐ number line

6. Represent the following mixed numbers.

points
/ 2

a. $1\frac{2}{10}$

b. $3\frac{3}{7}$

7. Measure the angles using a protractor and complete.

points
/ 2

a.

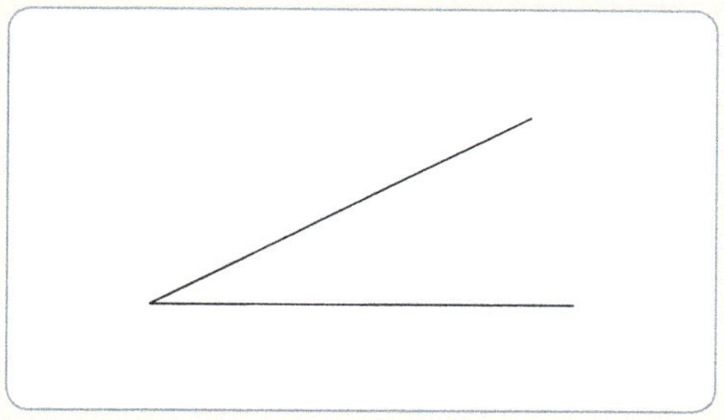

The angle is ______________.

b.

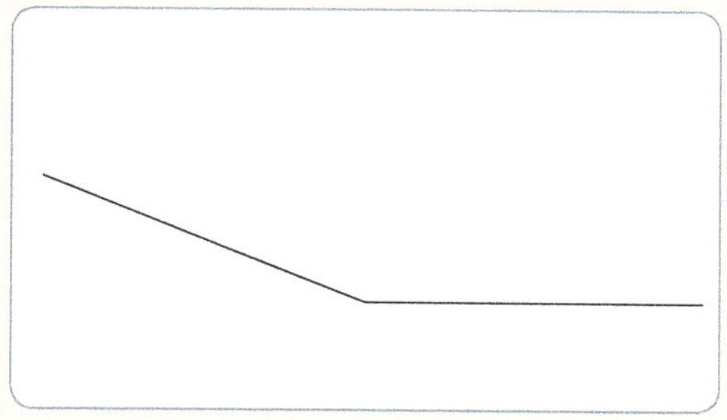

The angle is ______________.

8. Make the following angles using a protractor.

points
/ 2

a. A 52° angle.

b. A 139° angle.

9. Complete the following figures so that they are symmetrical.

points
/ 2

10. Reflect the figure.

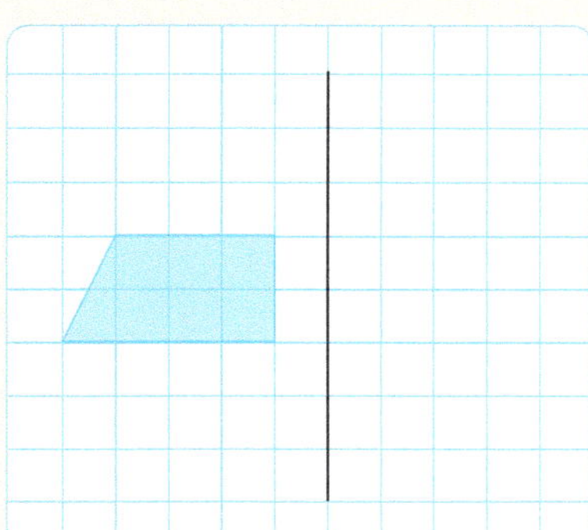

Mark the correct answer with an ✕ .

points
/ 4

11. Mandy has 15 fruits, 5 of which are bananas. What fraction do the bananas represent of all the fruits?

A. 5

B. 15

C. $\frac{5}{15}$

D. $\frac{5}{10}$

12. Which of the following fractions is read as eight-tenths?

A. $\frac{8}{12}$

B. $\frac{8}{10}$

C. $\frac{10}{8}$

D. $\frac{8}{100}$

13. What fraction is represented on the number line?

A. $\frac{3}{7}$

B. $\frac{4}{7}$

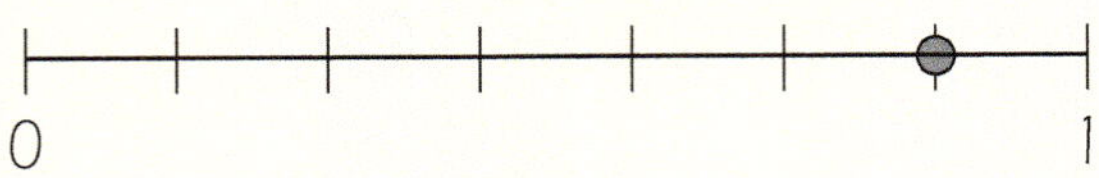

C. $\frac{5}{7}$

D. $\frac{6}{7}$

14. The angle in the image measures:

A. 90°.

B. More than 90°.

C. Less than 90°.

D. It can't be determined.

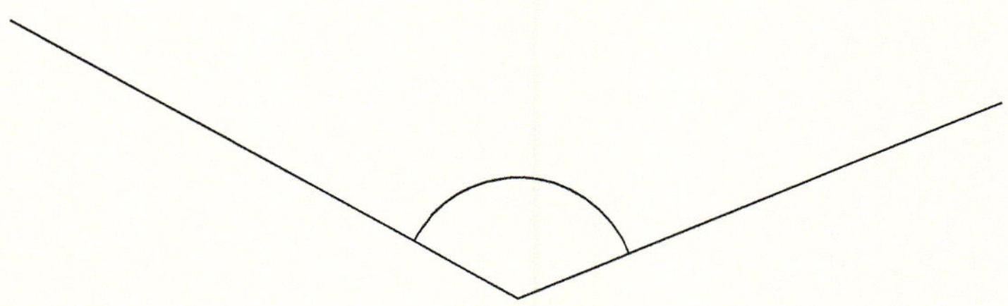

points

/2

15. What is the measurement of angle 1 compared to the measurement of angle 2?

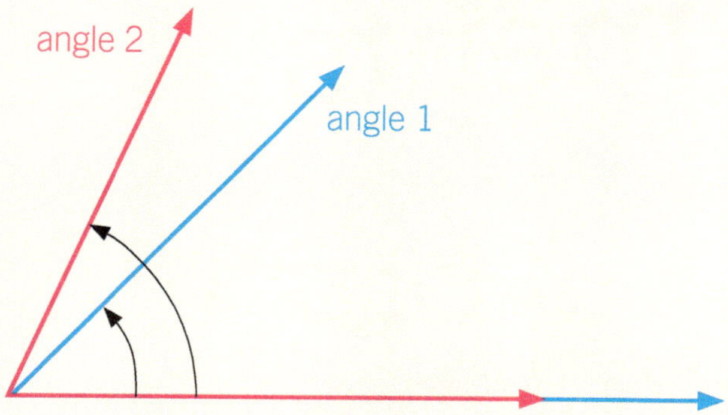

A. Greater than.

B. Less than.

C. Equal to.

D. You cannot compare.

16. Which option completes the figure making it symmetrical?

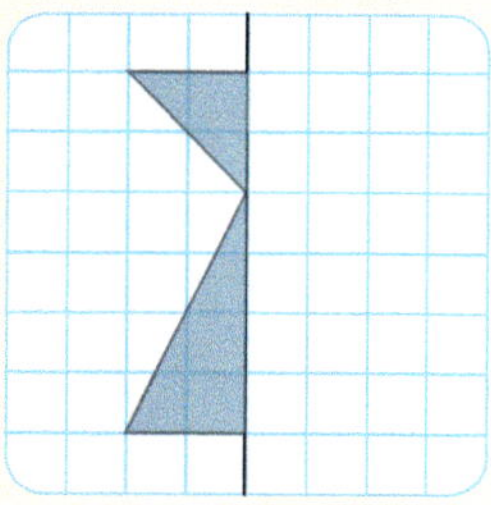

A.

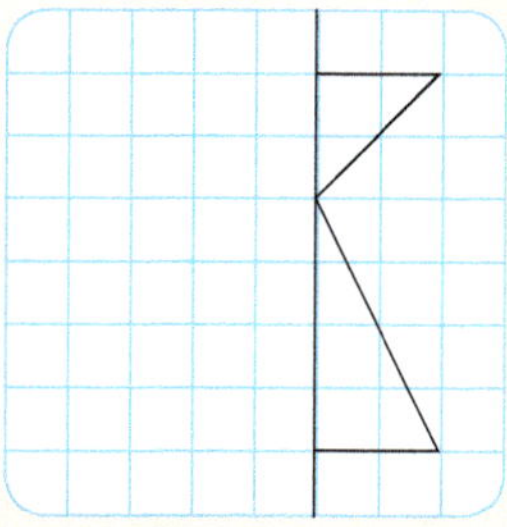

B.

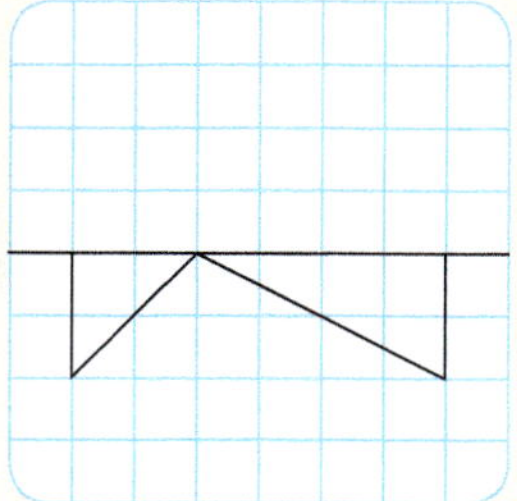

C.

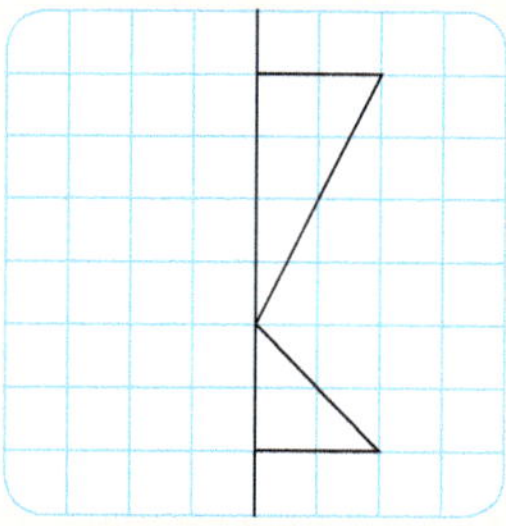

D.

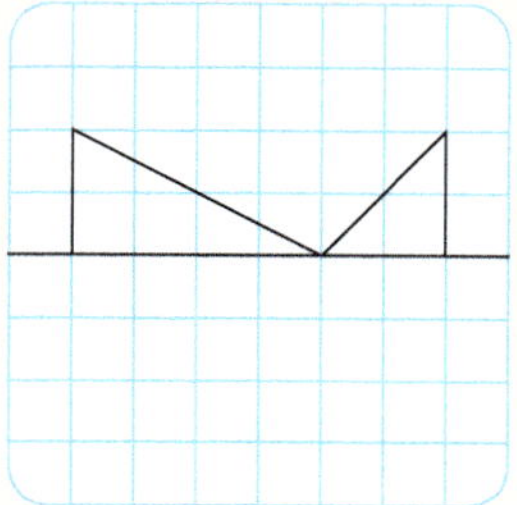

Find Test 4 Study Page

Unit 5

Measurements

One of the events performed in gymnastics is the floor exercise. In the event, gymnasts do a routine between 70 and 90 seconds long on a surface that is 12 meters long and 12 meters wide.

routine: a sequence of actions

Another event performed in gymnastics is the vault. The vault is a 135 centimeter high apparatus that gymnasts use to jump and flip into the air.

apparatus: piece of equipment

Key Words

analog

digital

establish

area

convert

In this unit you will learn to:

- read and record time on digital and analog clocks.
- determine equivalencies between years, months and hours.
- determine equivalencies between hours, minutes and seconds.
- measure length and convert units of measurement.
- calculate the area of squares and rectangles.
- be creative and precise when finding a solution to a problem.

What Do You Know? Initial Evaluation

Look at the information in the picture and answer.

1. How many seconds does the gymnast have left to finish her routine if it must be 80 seconds long?

2. What is the perimeter of the square where the gymnast performs her routine?

3. Compare your height with the height of the vault. Are you taller or shorter? By how much?

4. Why is teamwork so important in rowing?

____

____

____

Section
1 Measuring Time

Days, Months and Years

Connecting

On Saturday, April 20th, Nicholas marked his birthday on the calendar.

- How many years ago was Nicholas born?

___

- How many months are left before his next birthday? How did you figure this out?

___

___

- How many days are left before his next birthday?

___

Learning

January						
M	T	W	Th	F	Sa	S
	1	2	3	4	5	6
7	8	9	10	11	12	13
14	15	16	17	18	19	20
21	22	23	24	25	26	27
28	29	30	31			

A **month** can have 28, 30 or 31 days. For example, January has 31 days.

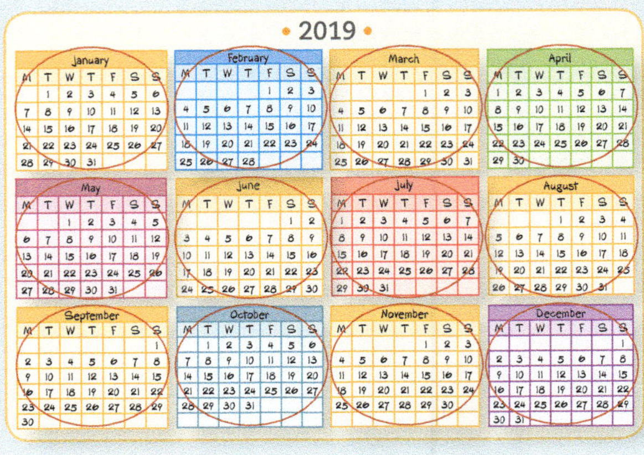

A **year** is **12 months** or **365 days** long.

Practicing

1. Look at the calendar in **Activity Card 2** and answer. Interpret

a. How many months equal half a year?

Half a year equals ☐ months.

b. How many days are there in the first 4 months of the year?

The first 4 months of the year are equal to ☐ days.

Did You Know...?

A semester is 6 months long and a trimester is 3. Since there are 12 months in a year, we can divide it into 2 semesters or 4 trimesters.

2. Read each situation and answer. Analyze

a. Amy is going on a trip in 3 months. What day will she leave?

September

M	T	W	T	F	S	S
						1
2	3	4	5	6	7	8
9	10	11	12	13	(14)	15
16	17	18	19	20	21	22
23	24	25	26	27	28	29
30						

today

October

M	T	W	T	F	S	S
	1	2	3	4	5	6
7	8	9	10	11	12	13
14	15	16	17	18	19	20
21	22	23	24	25	26	27
28	29	30	31			

November

M	T	W	T	F	S	S
				1	2	3
4	5	6	7	8	9	10
11	12	13	14	15	16	17
18	19	20	21	22	23	24
25	26	27	28	29	30	

December

M	T	W	T	F	S	S
						1
2	3	4	5	6	7	8
9	10	11	12	13	14	15
16	17	18	19	20	21	22
23	24	25	26	27	28	29
30	31					

She will leave on the ☐ of ☐.

b. My sister Julie will arrive from the United Kingdom in two and a half months. In how many days will I see her?

January

M	T	W	T	F	S	S
	1	2	3	4	5	6
7	8	9	10	11	12	13
14	15	16	17	(18)	19	20
21	22	23	24	25	26	27
28	29	30	31			

today

February

M	T	W	T	F	S	S
				1	2	3
4	5	6	7	8	9	10
11	12	13	14	15	16	17
18	19	20	21	22	23	24
25	26	27	28			

March

M	T	W	T	F	S	S
				1	2	3
4	5	6	7	8	9	10
11	12	13	14	15	16	17
18	19	20	21	22	23	24
25	26	27	28	29	30	31

April

M	T	W	T	F	S	S
1	2	3	4	5	6	7
8	9	10	11	12	13	14
15	16	17	18	19	20	21
22	23	24	25	26	27	28
29	30					

I will see her in ☐ days.

Time on Analog and Digital Clocks

Connecting

Kristin wakes up at six o'clock in the morning.

She starts school at eight thirty in the morning.

She goes to ballet class at six o'clock in the evening.

- Does Kristin wake up at the same time that she goes to ballet class? Explain.

____

____

____

Did You Know...?

If a timepiece is on a wall, it is a clock. If it is on your wrist, it is a watch.

Learning

Analog clocks have a **12-hour format** (format: design or arrangement). This means they divide the **day** into morning and afternoon/evening.

Digital clocks have either a **24-hour** or **12-hour format**. The 24-hour format is referred to as **military time**.

In the **12-hour format**, time from **midnight** to **noon** (noon: twelve o'clock midday) is written with **a.m.**, and time from noon to midnight with **p.m.**

Practicing

1. Write an appropriate time for each situation. Relate

2. Read the situation and complete each clock. Look at the example. Represent

The final game is at six o'clock in the evening.	06:00 PM	18:00	

a. My dentist appointment is at 5:30 in the afternoon. | : | : | 

b. My math class is at eleven o'clock in the morning. | : | : | 

c. My friend Larry will come to my house at 4:15 in the afternoon. | : | : | 

Seconds, Minutes and Hours

Connecting

In the school's track and field meet, Jeff, Chris, Paul and Sean ran the relay race.

- Which boy took the least amount of time to run his part of the relay race? Explain.

- Did the teams take more or less than a minute to complete the race? Explain.

Fun Fact!

At the 2012 Olympics in London, Jamaican runner Usain Bolt set an Olympic record for the 100 meter sprint. It took him 9.63 seconds to reach the finish line!

run at full speed

- How long did each team take to finish the race? Write their times as seconds and minutes.

Team 1 ▶ ☐ seconds, which equals ☐ minute and ☐ seconds.

Team 2 ▶ ☐ seconds, which equals ☐ minute and ☐ seconds.

Learning

Hours, **minutes** and **seconds** are units used to measure time. The following equivalencies can be established between them:

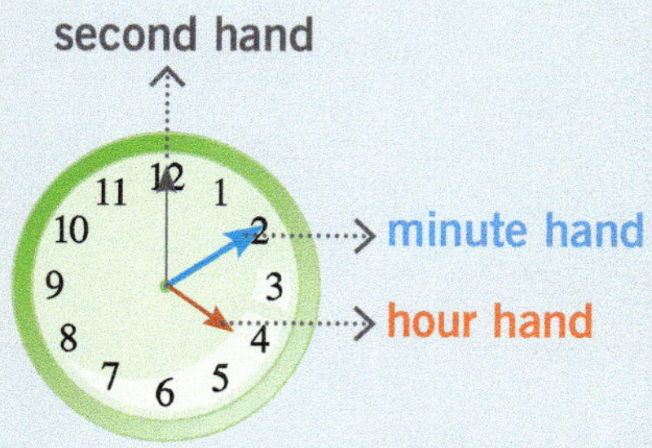

When the **hour hand** makes a complete circle, 12 hours have passed, which equals half of a day. Two full turns equal 1 day or 24 hours.

When the **minute hand** makes a complete circle, 60 minutes have passed, which equals 1 hour.

When the **second hand** makes a complete circle, 60 seconds have passed, which equals 1 minute.

To establish equivalencies, use these operations:

hours ➡ minutes ➡ seconds (multiply by 60, multiply by 60)

hours ⬅ minutes ⬅ seconds (divide by 60, divide by 60)

Example:
3 hours equal 180 minutes because
60 + 60 + 60 ▶ 3 times 60
$3 \times 60 = 180$

Example:
240 seconds equal 4 minutes because
$240 \div 60 = 4$

Practicing

1. Complete the following equivalencies. Apply

a. 2 minutes equal ____ seconds

b. 120 seconds equal ____ minutes

c. 2 hours equal ____ minutes

d. 420 minutes equal ____ hours

e. half an hour equals ____ minutes

Did You Know...?

The symbol for hours is **h**, **min** is for minutes and **s** is for seconds.

2. Look at the clocks and write how much time has passed. Apply

a. 

→ 

______ minutes have passed.

b. 

p.m.
→ 

p.m.

______ hours and ______ minutes have passed.

c. 

→ 

______ hours and ______ minutes have passed.

3. Write an activity you can do in the given amount of time. Follow the example. Interpret

5 seconds → tie my shoes

a. 45 minutes → ______________________

b. 1 hour and 24 minutes → ______________________

c. 12 seconds → ______________________

d. 120 minutes → ______________________

4. Read the word problem and answer. Interpret

Maria is competing in the Calculus Olympiad. She has three minutes to solve a problem and can see the time she has left on the clock.

a. How many seconds have passed since she started?

b. How many seconds does she have left to answer?

Quiz Yourself

Read the situation and answer.

Lucy lives in Seattle, and she will visit her grandmother in Chicago. The trip takes 1 day and 22 hours by bus. She bought this ticket:

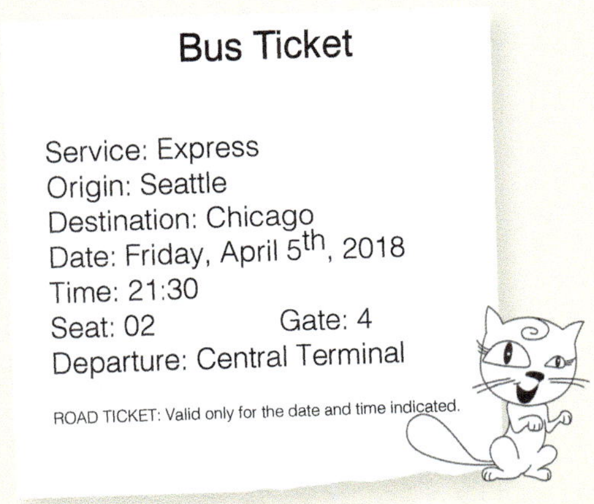
Bus Ticket

Service: Express
Origin: Seattle
Destination: Chicago
Date: Friday, April 5th, 2018
Time: 21:30
Seat: 02 Gate: 4
Departure: Central Terminal

ROAD TICKET: Valid only for the date and time indicated.

- What day and at what time will Lucy arrive in Chicago?

Answer: ______________________________

____

Measuring Length

Centimeters and Meters

Connecting

The P.E. teacher is recording the height of all of his students.

- What are the teacher and the students doing? What measuring instrument are they using?

____

____

- Is it the same to say that Mike is **134 centimeters** tall and that he is **1 meter and 34 centimeters** tall? Explain.

____

____

- How many centimeters equal one meter?

____

Education through Values

movements of the body

We can communicate in different ways, for example, by using gestures, by speaking or by writing. Throughout history, people have communicated through signals, drawings and writings. Nowadays, we also communicate through new technologies.

Learning

Centimeters (cm) and **meters (m)** are **standardized** units of measurement.
1 meter equals **100 centimeters**.

Example: Felicity's mother is 1 meter and 60 centimeters, or 160 centimeters tall.

To **establish equivalencies** you can use these operations:

multiply by 100	divide by 100
meters ➡ centimeters	centimeters ➡ meters
3 meters equal 300 centimeters, 100 + 100 + 100 ▶ 3 times 100; $3 \times 100 = 300$	500 centimeters equal 5 meters because $500 \div 100 = 5$.

Practicing

1. Write the heights in two different ways. Follow the example. Apply

a.

b.

Example	a.	b.
1 meter and 5 centimeters		
105 centimeters		

Remember!

Start from 0 when you measure with a ruler or a tape measure.

Challenge

Measure your friends! Who is the tallest? Put yourselves in order from shortest to tallest.

Conversion Word Problems

Connecting

- What question does Laura want to answer?

  ____

- What information does she have? In what units of measurement is it expressed?

  ____

- In what units of measurement should she express her answer?

  ____

- What strategy does Amelia use to answer? Explain.

  ____

- What strategy would you use to answer Laura's question? Explain how you would do it.

  ____

  ____

Learning

When you are solving **unit of measurement conversion word problems**, you must consider the unit of measurement in which the **information** is given, as well as the unit of measurement you have to express the **answer** in.

Read the **word problem** and select the **information** you need in order to answer the **question**.

A snake can be up to two and a half meters long.

How many centimeters does that equal?

Two and a half meters long.
Information expressed in meters.

Choose a **strategy** to answer the question.

Two and a half meters is the same as
2 meters and 50 centimeters.
2 meters equals 200 centimeters.

$2 \times 100 = 200$
50 cm + 200 cm = 250 cm
A snake can be up to 250 centimeters long.

Answer the question in the **unit of measurement asked for.**

Practicing

1. Identify the unit of measurement in which the information is expressed and the unit of measurement you have to express the answer in. Identify

a. A giraffe's neck can be up to 2 meters long. If a giraffe is approximately 6 meters tall, how many centimeters long is the rest of a giraffe's body?

Unit of measurement of information ▶ ____________ Unit of measurement of answer ▶ ____________

b. A giant female tortoise can be up to 90 cm long. On the other hand, a giant male tortoise can be up to 120 cm long. How much longer in centimeters is a male tortoise than a female tortoise?

Unit of measurement of information ▶ ____________ Unit of measurement of answer ▶ ____________

2. Solve the word problems. Apply

a. Sofia's brother was 93 cm tall two years ago. Now he is 108 cm tall. How many centimeters has he grown?

Information and its units of measurement: →

Strategy used to answer: →

Answer in the units of measurement asked for: →

b. Mrs. Evans is making a dress for her daughter. She bought two and a half meters of fabric. How many centimeters of fabric did she buy?

Information and its units of measurement: →

Strategy used to answer: →

Answer in the units of measurement asked for: →

c. Thomas measured the length of the classroom's whiteboard using his handspan. If his handspan is 10 cm and the length of the whiteboard is 20 hand spans, how many meters long is the whiteboard?

Information and its units of measurement: ➡ ______________________________

Strategy used to answer: ➡

Answer in the units of measurement asked for: ➡ ______________________________

Quiz Yourself

Do the following activity.

1st Measure the length of the classroom with your feet.

How many long is the classroom? ▶ ☐ .

2nd Measure the length of your foot with a ruler.

How many centimeters long is your ? ▶ ☐ cm.

3rd Use the information to calculate the length of the classroom and express it in centimeters and meters.

Length in centimeters:

Length in meters:

Let's Check!

Days, Months and Years

1. Answer using the information in the picture.

points ___ / 3

My Family's Birthdays!

• March 13th	Dad (45 years old)
• May 26th	Sister (16 years old)
• June 3rd	Grandma (75 years old)
• August 1st	Me (Ellen) (9 years old)
• September 15th	Mom (45 years old)
• November 10th	Grandpa (77 years old)

a. How many days are there between Ellen's birthday and her Grandpa's?

▶ ______________________

b. In how many years will Ellen's dad be the same age as her grandma is now?

▶ ______________________

c. How old is Ellen in months? ▶ ______________________

Time on Analog and Digital Clocks

2. Match each situation with the most appropriate time.

points ___ / 4

a. family dinner

b. doing homework

c. recess

d. getting up to go to school

07:00

10:00 AM

7:30 PM

Seconds, Minutes and Hours

3. Read the situation and answer.

points: /2

A movie theater has 2 theaters with a movie showing in each.

	Schedule	
Theater 1	10:00 – 11:45	12:00 – 13:45
Theater 2	10:30 – 12:30	12:45 – 14:45

a. How many minutes long is the movie in Theater 1? ▶ ______ minutes.

b. Compare the movies in Theater 1 and Theater 2. Which one lasts longer? What is the difference in minutes between the two movies?

____

Conversion Word Problems

4. Read the word problem and answer.

points: /3

Hannah, Ethan and Natalie threw the discus in P.E. class and reached the following distances: Hannah, 8 meters; Ethan, 6 meters and 30 centimeters; and Natalie, 5 and a half meters. How far in centimeters did each student reach?

Information and its units of measurement: ➡ ______________________________

Strategy to answer: ➡

Answer in the units of measurement asked for: ➡ ______________________________

Area of a Two-Dimensional Figure

Connecting

Amelia and Jim are making a big jigsaw puzzle, and they want to know how many pieces they have left to finish it.

- How many pieces fit along the width of the puzzle? ▶ ____________
- How many pieces fit along the length of the puzzle? ▶ ____________
- How many pieces do they need to finish the puzzle? ▶ ____________

Remember!

The **perimeter** is the total distance around a shape.

- How many pieces are in the puzzle? Explain how you got your answer.

____

____

- How are the number of pieces that fit along the length and the width of the puzzle related to the total number of puzzle pieces?

____

____

Learning

The **area** of a two-dimensional figure is the measurement of its **surface**.
In order to calculate the area of a figure, use a specific unit of measurement and count the number of times that measurement is repeated in the figure.

Example:

The figure:

Specific unit of measurement:

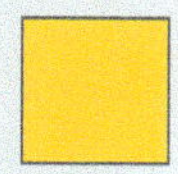

Times the unit of measurement is in the figure:

The area of the figure is 12 .

Practicing

1. Calculate the area of the following figures using as a unit of measurement. Apply

a.

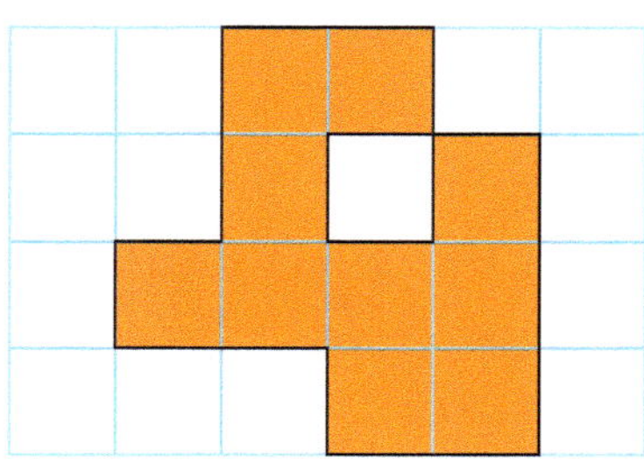

Area ▸ ____________ .

b.

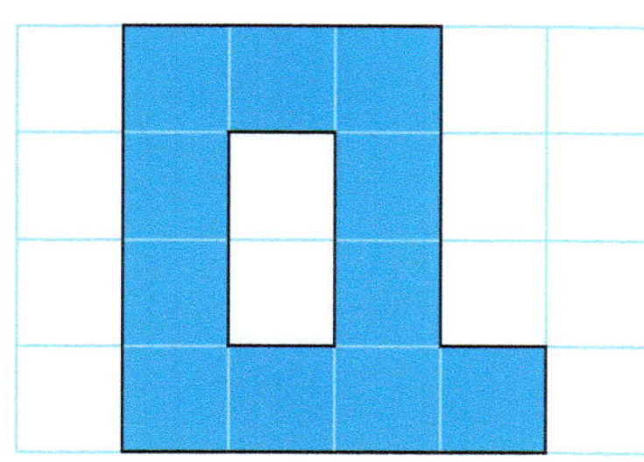

Area ▸ ____________ .

c.

Area ▸ ____________ .

2. Calculate the area of the following figures using as a unit of measurement. Apply

a.

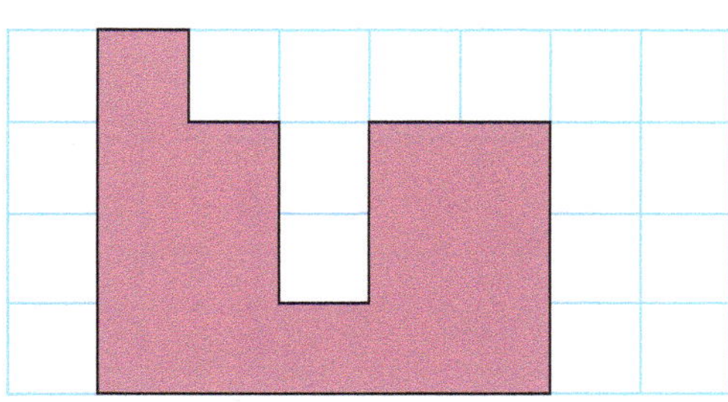

Area ▸ ____________ .

b.

Area ▸ ____________ .

Different Figures with Equal Areas

Connecting

Liz, Jake and Anthony have been given 5 identical squares to make a figure.

- What is the area of each figure using □ as the unit of measurement?

Area of 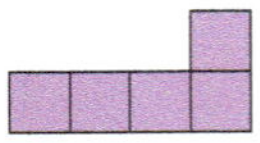 ▶ __________ □.

Area of 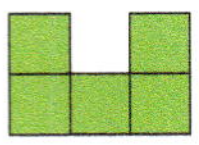 ▶ __________ □.

Area of  ▶ __________ □.

- Why is it possible to create different figures with the same area? Explain.

____

____

Did You Know...?

These figures are **pentominos**. A pentomino is a figure made up of 5 squares connected by at least one edge. You can make 12 different pentominos.

Learning

Some figures look **different** but have the **same area**.

Example:

rectangle 1 rectangle 2

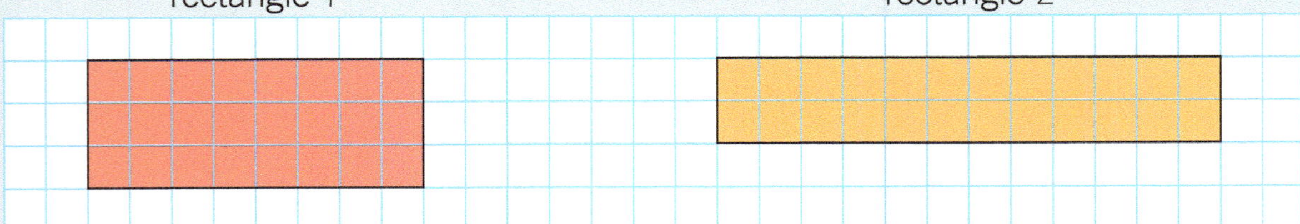

The rectangles look **different**, but both have an **area** of 24 □.

Practicing

1. Match the rectangles that have the same area. Relate

a.

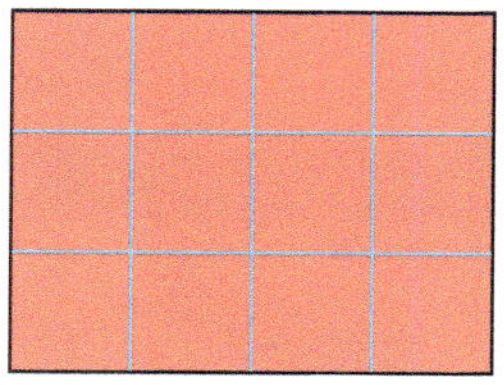

b.

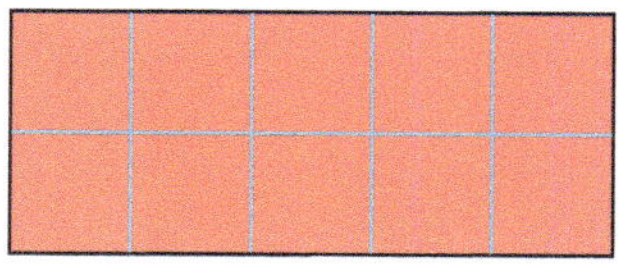

c.

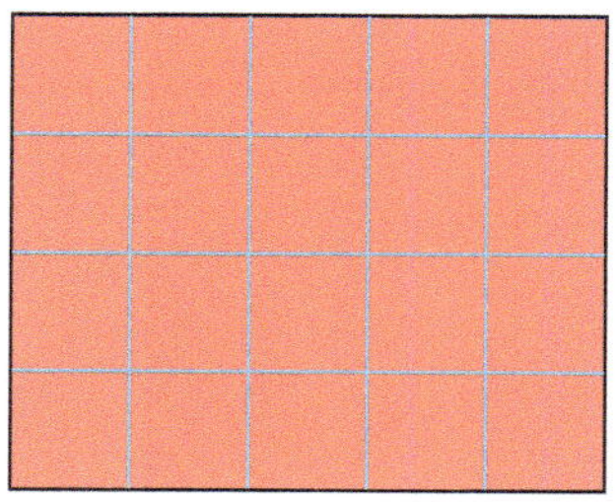

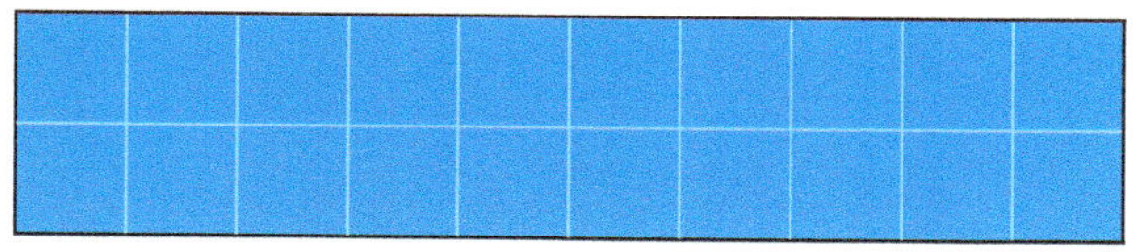

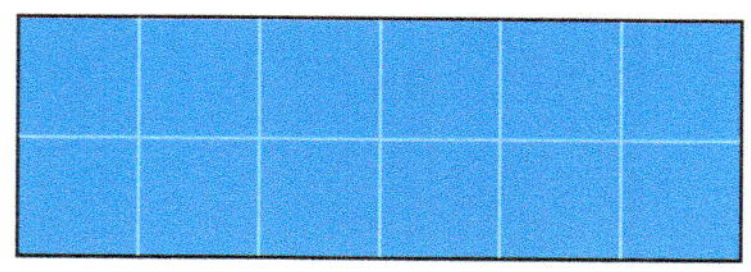

2. Calculate the area of the rectangles. Then draw a different rectangle that has the same area as the first one on the grid. Use ☐ as a unit of measurement. Apply

a.

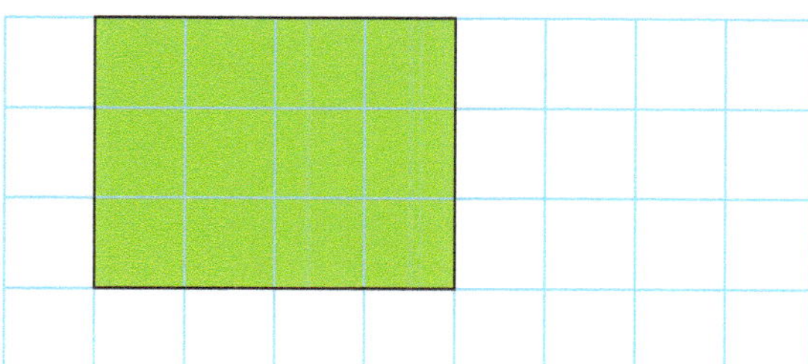

Area ▶ ____________ ☐.

Area ▶ ____________ ☐.

b.

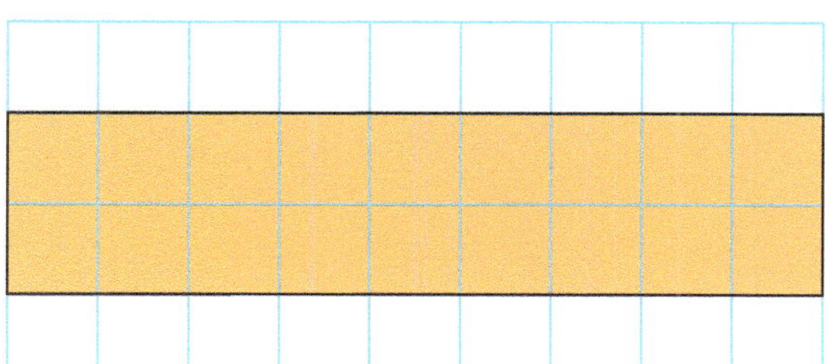

Area ▶ ____________ ☐.

Area ▶ ____________ ☐.

Square Centimeters and Meters

Connecting

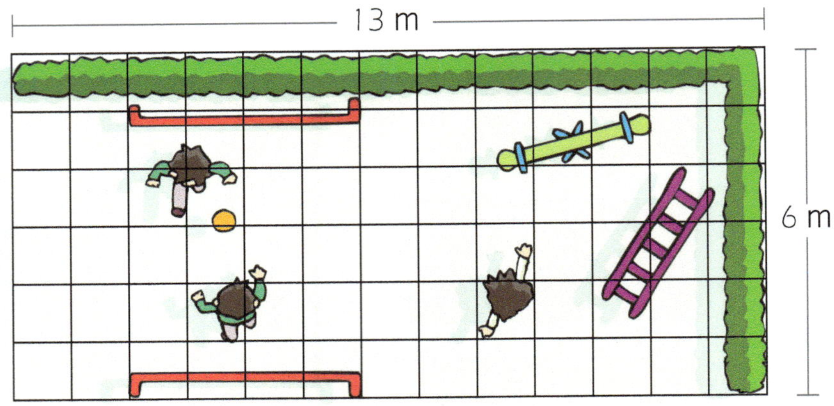

Ethan drew his backyard in the following grid so he could calculate its area.

- How many squares represent the length and width of the backyard?

Length ▶ ________ ☐.

Width ▶ ________ ☐.

- How long is each side of the square on the grid? Explain how you calculated it.

____

- Could you use squares with 1 cm sides on the grid? Explain.

____

Tip

Read **cm²** as "square centimeters" and **m²** as "square meters."

Learning

To measure surfaces you must choose a **unit of measurement.** It will vary depending on the size of the surface you are measuring.

If you are measuring **small surfaces**, like notebooks or tiles, use square centimeters (cm^2).

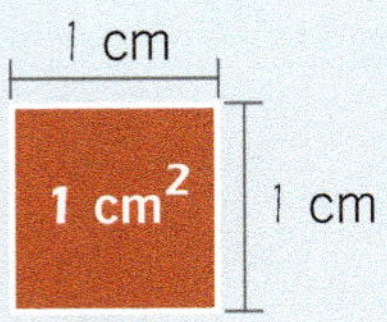

If you are measuring **big surfaces**, like a room or a soccer field, use square meters (m^2).

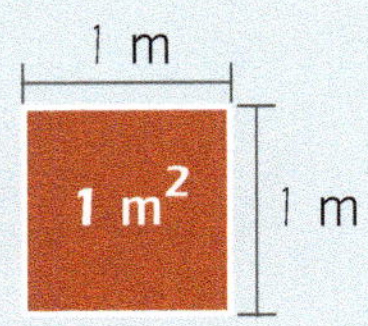

Practicing

1. Color the most appropriate unit of measurement to calculate the size of the surfaces. Understand

a.

cm^2 m^2

b.

cm^2 m^2

c.

cm^2 m^2

d.

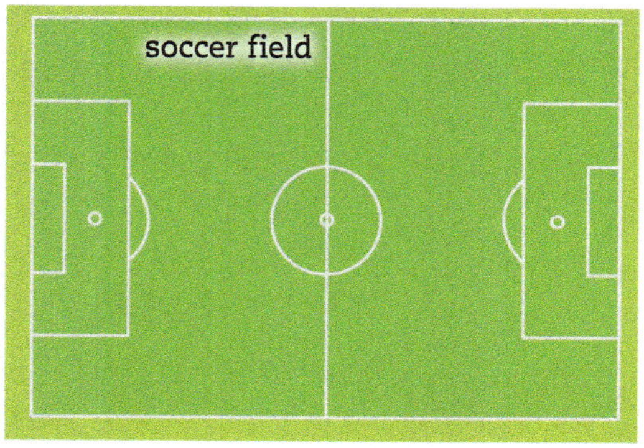

cm^2 m^2

2. Complete each sentence with the correct unit of measurement. Understand

a. The wall I have to paint has an area of 10 ______________.

b. Ralph measured the area of a piece of paper, and it was 100 ______________.

c. The fabric she bought to make curtains had an area of 2 ______________.

d. The area of the picture with Courtney and Patricia is 130 ______________.

Area of Rectangles and Squares

Connecting

Maggie and her mother want to know the area of their vegetable garden.

- Explain, in your own words, what Maggie means.

____

- How long and how wide is the vegetable garden? ▸ __________ and __________ .
- What is the area of the space where they built the garden? ▸ __________
- How is the length and the width related to the area of the garden? Explain.

____

Did You Know...?

In the U.S. land is measured in **acres**. One acre equals 4,047 m².

Learning

To calculate the **area of a square or rectangle**, multiply length times width.

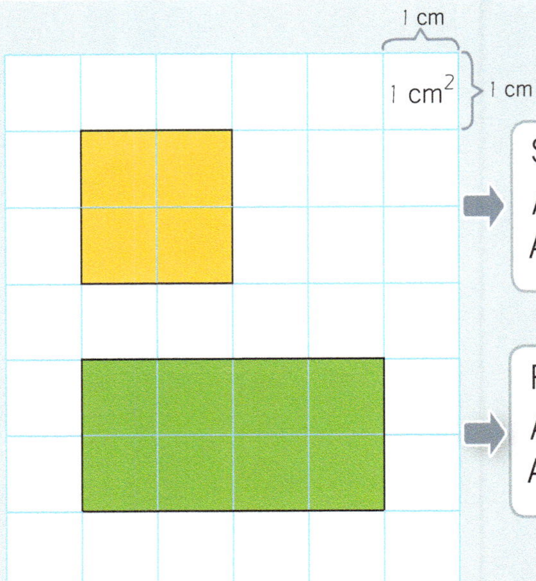

Square:
Area ▸ length multiplied by width
Area ▸ 2 cm × 2 cm = 4 cm^2

Rectangle:
Area ▸ length multiplied by width
Area ▸ 4 cm × 2 cm = 8 cm^2

Practicing

1. Calculate the area of the figures. Apply

a.

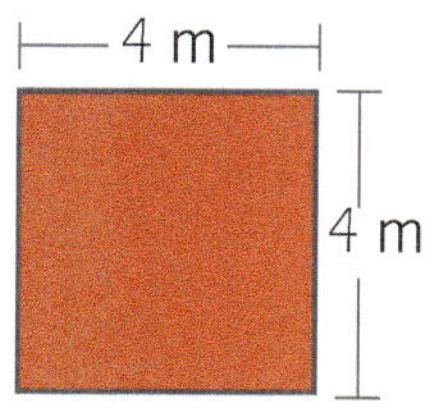

Length ▶ ____________

Width ▶ ____________

Area ▼

b.

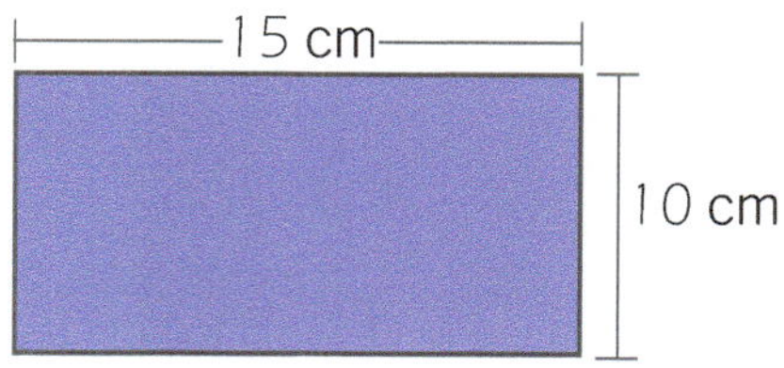

Length ▶ ____________

Width ▶ ____________

Area ▼

2. Consider the measurement of the squares in each grid. Then calculate the area of the figures. Apply

a.

Length ▶ ____________ Width ▶ ____________

Area ▶

b.

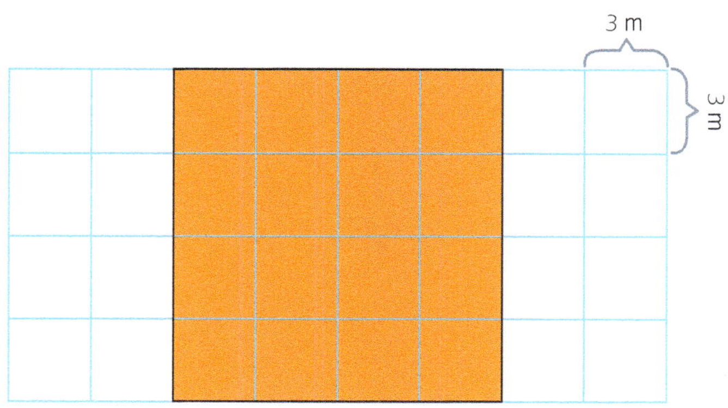

Length ▶ ____________ Width ▶ ____________

Area ▶

c.

Length ▶ ____________ Width ▶ ____________

Area ▶

Quiz Yourself

Read the situation and answer.

Freddy built a 1 m^2 wall so he can paint a mural on it. He wants to draw square paintings with 15 cm sides as part of the mural.

- How many paintings, side by side, can he draw as part of the mural? Use the grid to help you.

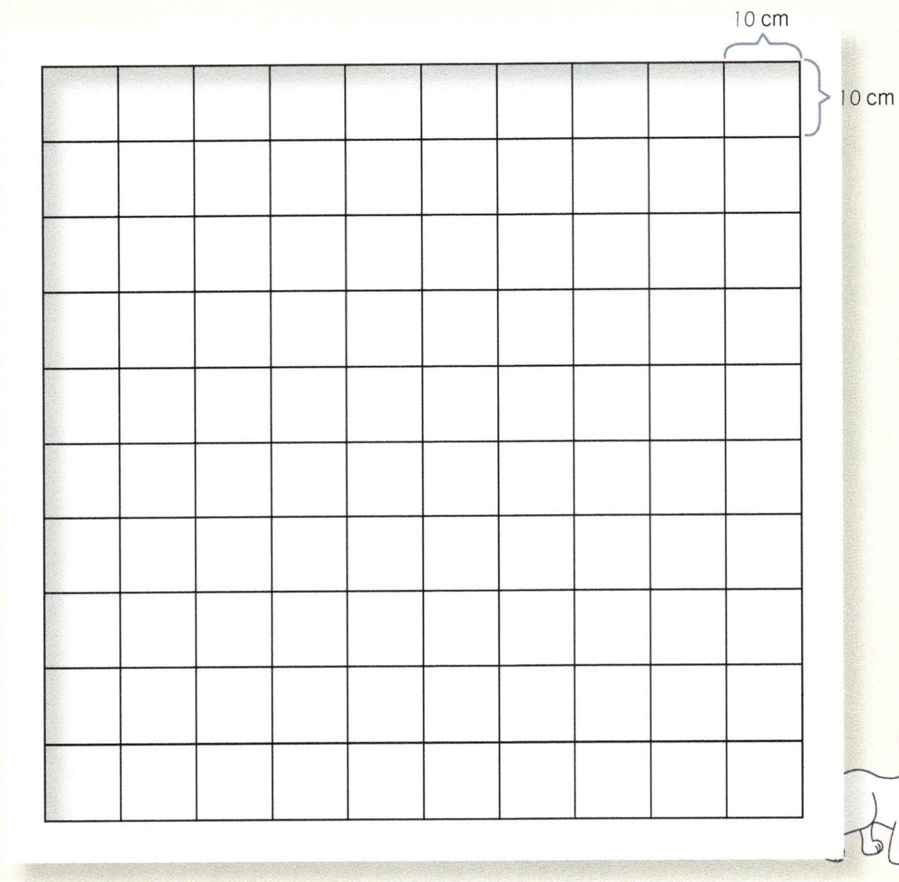

Did You Know...?

One of the largest murals in the world is in Dubai. It's visible from the sky!

Freddy can draw ________________ paintings on the wall.

- Was Freddy able to cover the whole wall with his paintings? Explain.

____

____

Exam Strategies

Multiple-Choice Questions

1. Which of the following figures has the greatest area?

A. 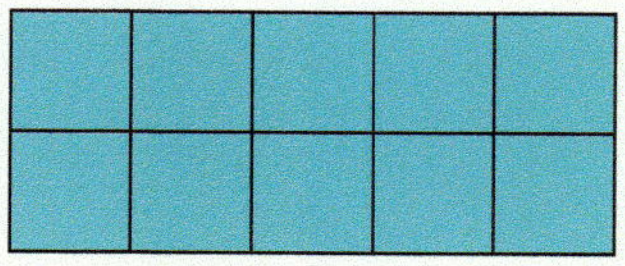

C. 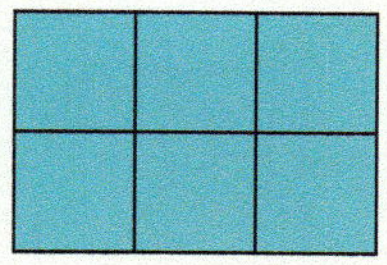

B. 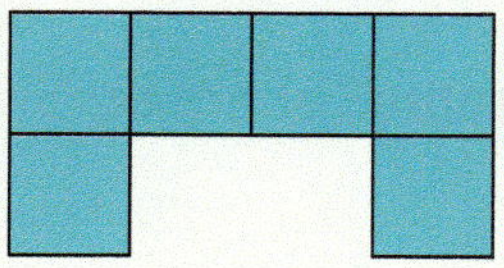

D. 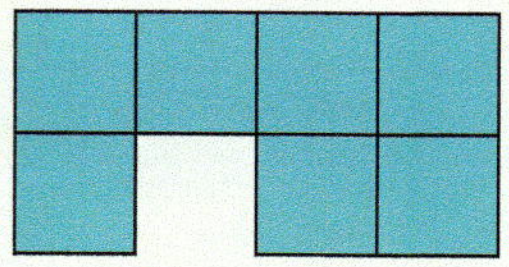

Analyzing the Answers

A. In this case, the area is 10 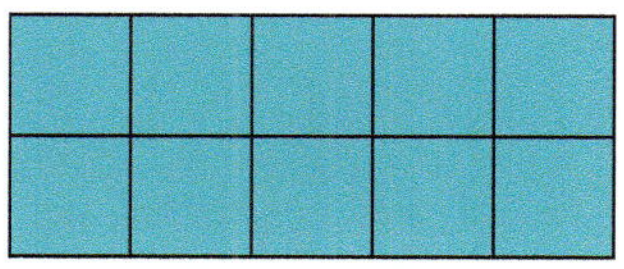 .

B. In this case, the area is 6 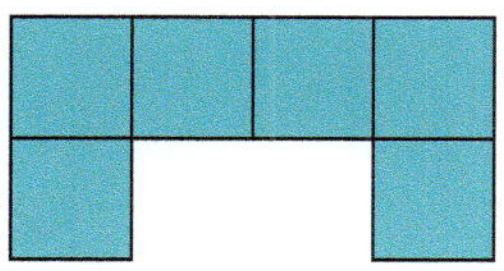, so it has less area than figures A and D.

C. In this case, the area is 6 , so it has the same area as figure B.

D. In this case, the area is 7 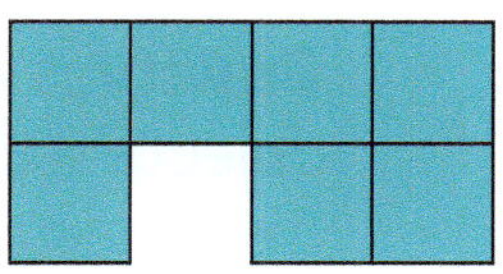, so it has a greater area than figures B and C but has less area than figure A.

▸ Therefore, **A** is the correct answer.

1. A B C D

Section 4 Mass

Grams and Kilograms

Connecting

- How many kilograms (kg) is the bag of flour?

  It is ____ kg.

- How many grams (g) is the bag of flour?

  It is ____ g.

- Therefore, how many grams (g) are equivalent to 1 kilogram (kg)?

  1 kg is equivalent to ____ g.

Learning

Mass quantifies the amount of matter a body or object has. To measure mass, you can use an analog scale. The **units of measurement** for mass are **kilograms (kg)** and **grams (g)**. Some of their equivalences are:

1 kg = 1,000 g $\quad \frac{1}{2}$ kg = 500 g $\quad \frac{1}{4}$ kg = 250 g

Did You Know...?

People often confuse mass and weight. When you "weigh" yourself, you are measuring your mass and the gravitational force.

Word Focus

Gravity is a force that pulls two objects toward each other. It acts like a magnet. Gravity is what keeps us on the ground and not floating in the air!

Practicing

1. Look at the shopping list and answer. Interpret

a. How many grams of cheese are they going to buy?

☐ g of cheese.

b. What product are they buying $\frac{1}{2}$ kg of?

____

c. Which products are they going to buy the same amount of?

____

2. Look at the image and answer by explaining your ideas. Analyze

a. Is Jenny correct?

____

____

b. What do you think her body mass is?

____

____

3. Circle the correct answer and support your choice in each case. Evaluate

a. Which fruit should be expressed in grams?

Explain: ______________________________

____

____

b. Which fruit should be expressed in kilograms?

Explain: ______________________________

____

____

More or Less Mass

Connecting

- What is the mass of  ?

  The mass of the notebook is ______ g.

- Which notebook has **more** mass? Circle it.

- How did you know which notebook has more mass? Explain.

____

____

____

- Considering the mass of both notebooks, which relationship is correct? Circle it.

<

>

Learning

To compare the mass of two objects you can:

- Measure them **informally** by taking one object in each hand and identifying which one is heavier.
- Use a **scale**. If it is a balance, the side that the scale inclines toward will hold the object with more mass. If it is an analog scale, first measure the mass of one object, and then that of the other, and compare.

balance

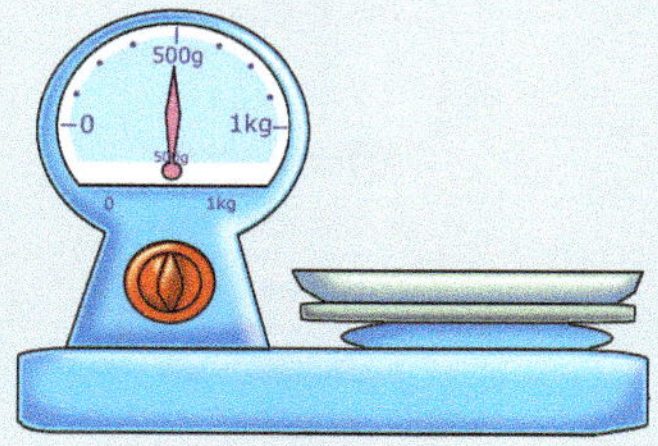

analog scale

Practicing

1. Answer. Analyze

a. Which of these has **the most** mass? Circle it.

1,200 g

1 kg

$\frac{3}{4}$ kg

800 g

b. Which of these has **the least** mass? Circle it.

c. Robert says that 1 kg of stones has more mass than 1,000 g of feathers. Is he right? Explain.

____

____

What Did You Learn?

Final Evaluation

1. Match each digital clock with the correct analog clock.

points ___ / 5

a. 13:00

b. 16:30

c. 21:30

d. 11:00 AM

e. 5:00 PM

2. Read each word problem and write the correct equivalence.

points ___ / 2

a. If a decade is 10 years, how many months is that equal to?

A decade is equal to __________ months.

b. Randy takes 1 and a half minutes to run around the soccer field. If he is running at the same speed, how many seconds will it take him to run around the soccer field 2 times?

Randy will take __________ seconds to run around the field twice.

3. Solve the following word problem.

points

/ 3

During the javelin throw at a track and field meet, Eric's throw reached 4 m and 30 cm, and David's throw reached 3 m and 15 cm. What is the difference in centimeters between their throws?

Information and the unit of measurement: ➡ ______________________

____

Strategy used to answer: ➡

Answer in the unit of measurement asked for: ➡ ______________________

____

4. Calculate the area of each figure, using ☐ as the unit of measurement.

points

/ 2

a.

Area ▶ ______________ ☐.

b.

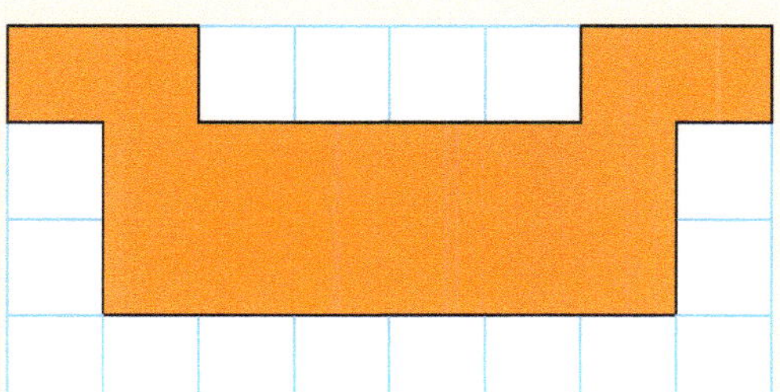

Area ▶ ______________ ☐.

Mark the correct answer with an ✕ .

points
/ 4

5. Brenda starts school at 8:30 in the morning. At which time should she wake up?

   A. 6:30 p.m.

   B. 6:30 a.m.

   C. 8:00 p.m.

   D. 9:00 p.m.

6. Approximately how many days are there in half a year?

   A. 90 days

   B. 180 days

   C. 300 days

   D. 360 days

7. Mindy's favorite TV show lasts 1 hour and 30 minutes. How long is the show in minutes?

   A. 130 minutes

   B. 100 minutes

   C. 90 minutes

   D. 60 minutes

8. Nathan and Amy made a tape measure that was two and a half meters long. How many centimeters long is the tape measure?

   A. 250 cm

   B. 230 cm

   C. 200 cm

   D. 180 cm

9. What is the area of the following figure if each  is 1 m^2?

points
2

A. 3 m^2

B. 6 m^2

C. 9 m^2

D. 12 m^2

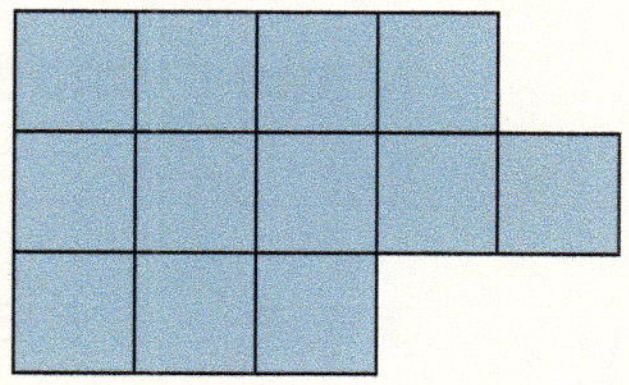

10. Which of the rectangles has the same area as the rectangle below?

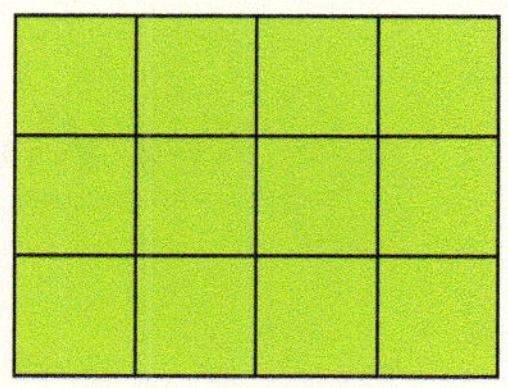

A.

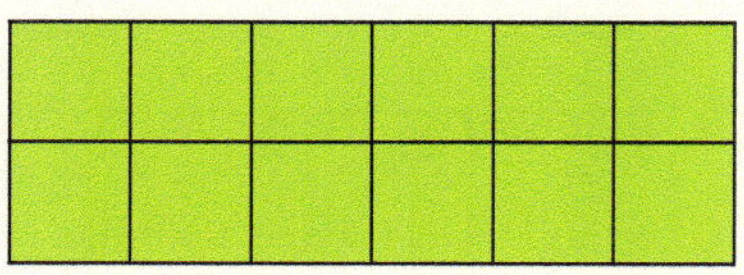

B.

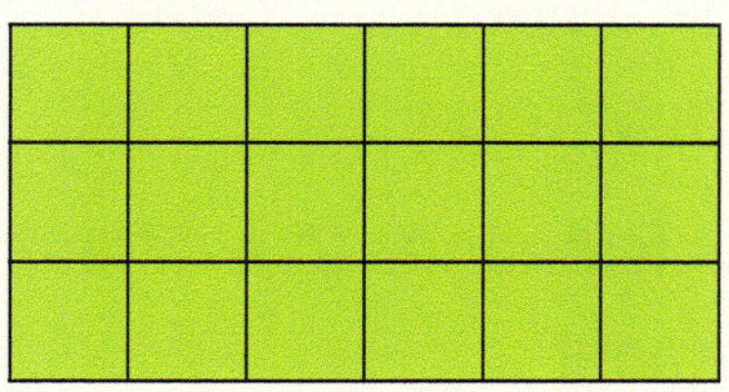

C.

D.

Find Test 5 Study Page

Glossary

4.1 Key Words Unit 1

ten thousand – *n*, one with 4 zeros

hundred thousand – *n*, one with 5 zeros

number line – *n*, a line with marks that show values where numbers can be represented

4.2 Key Words Unit 2

survey – *n*, a method of gathering information

population – *n*, the entire group from which a sample is taken

sample – *n*, a smaller selection of a larger population or group used to study its characteristics

4.3 Key Words Unit 3

million – *n*, one with 6 zeros; one thousand thousands

interval – *n*, the distance between two points

4.4 Key Words Unit 4

fraction – *n*, a number like $\frac{1}{2}$ or $\frac{5}{8}$ that represents the parts taken from the whole

part-whole – *n*, a representation that shows a relationship between a part and its whole

mixed number – *n*, a whole number and a fraction

whole number – *n*, a number that is not a fraction and is not negative

angle – *n*, the space between two straight lines that have a common point

line of symmetry – *n*, an imaginary line that divides a symmetrical shape in half

4.5 Key Words Unit 5

analog – *adj*, referring to a clock that has hour and minute hands

digital – *adj*, showing time with numbers, not with hour and minute hands

establish – *v*, to determine

area – *n*, the amount of space inside a shape, room or region

convert – *v*, to change to a different system of measurement

A

a.m. – *adj*, from 12 midnight to 12 noon

analog scale – *n*, an instrument with a gauge or electronic display used for weighing

antique – *adj*, an older, valuable object that is often collected

apparatus – *n*, a piece of equipment

auction house – *n*, a company that runs public sales where items are sold to people who offer to pay the most money

B

balance – *n*, an instrument with pans of equal weight on two ends used for weighing

bar chart – *n*, a chart that uses horizontal or vertical bars to show data

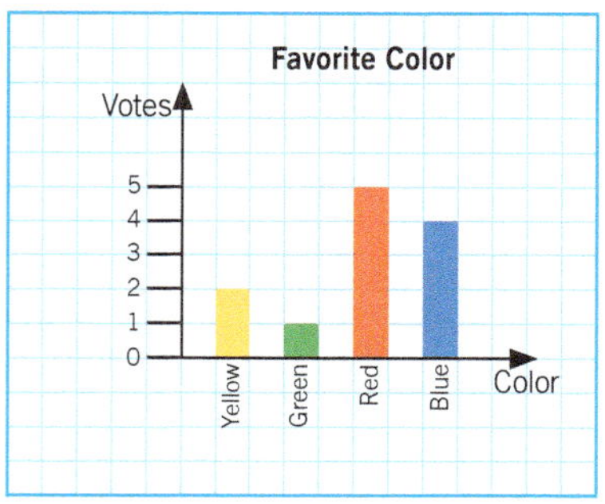

C

campaign – *n*, an activity designed to produce a particular result

coed – *adj*, having both male and female members

collectible – *adj*, considered valuable or important by people to save

composition – *n*, writing numbers by putting digits from 0 to 9 in the correct position according to place value

consumption – *n*, the eating or using up of something

D

decomposition – *n*, a way to write numbers by showing the value of each digit

denominator – *n*, the number at the bottom of a fraction with the parts of the whole fraction

$$\frac{1}{17}$$

digit – *n*, a written symbol for the numbers 0 to 9

divide – *v*, to calculate how many times a number contains another number

E

estimate – *v*, to find an answer that is close to the exact amount

evaporate – *v*, to change from liquid to vapor

expensive – *adj*, having a high price

G

grid – *n*, paper with fine lines that make up a regular arrangement

H

hour hand – *n*, the short hand that marks the hours on a clock or watch

L

life span – *n*, the length of time something functions

M

mass – *n*, the measure of how much matter an object has

mile – *n*, a unit of length equal to about 1.61 kilometers

minute hand – *n*, the long hand that marks the minutes on a clock or watch

mural – *n*, a painting on a wall

N

numerator – *n*, the number on top of a fraction that signals how many parts of the whole fraction there are

$$\frac{1}{7}$$

O

oar – *n*, a long pole with a flat and wide end used for rowing or steering a boat

P

P.E. – *n*, abbreviation for physical education; a class where sports and exercise are taught

pentomino – *n*, a geometric shape made by joining five squares together side by side

perimeter – *n*, the total distance around a figure

pictograph – *n*, a chart that uses symbols

place value chart – *n*, a chart that divides digits of a number into their place values

82,000				
TTh	Th	H	T	O
8	2	0	0	0

p.m. – *adj*, from 12 noon to 12 midnight

protractor – *n*, a semicircular tool used for measuring angles

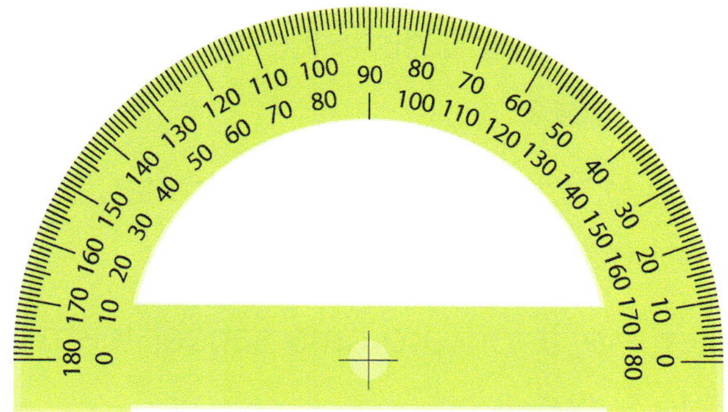

puzzle – *n*, a question, problem or game that requires thinking to be answered or solved

R

random – *adj*, not able to be predicted; happening by chance

random sample – *n*, a group that is chosen by chance from the larger population

recreational – *adj*, done for fun, pleasure or enjoyment

reference – *v*, to mention or use something else

routine – *n*, a sequence of actions

S

second hand – *n*, a third hand of a clock or watch that moves to show seconds

semicircle – *n*, half of a circle

set – *n*, a group or collection of something

sprint – *n*, a short distance race run at a very fast speed

stock – *n*, a liquid made from meat, fish or vegetables used for soup

striker – *n*, a forward on a soccer team who tries to score goals

T

table – *n*, a collection of information arranged in rows and columns

tablespoon – *n*, a spoon used by cooks to measure dry and liquid ingredients; about 15 milliliters

tape measure – *n*, a piece of cloth, metal or plastic used for measuring length

thousand – *n*, the natural number following 999 and before 1,001

timepiece – *n*, a clock or watch

tournament – *n*, a series of contests between many teams or competitors who compete for a final prize

triangle – *n*, a thin flat piece of plastic or metal in the shape of a triangle used in technical drawing

two-dimensional – *adj*, having only two dimensions, length and width

Place Value Chart

Example: 734,253

HTh	TTh	Th	H	T	O
(hundred thousands)	(ten thousands)	(thousands)	(hundreds)	(tens)	(ones)
7	3	4	2	5	3

Math Symbols

plus	$+$
minus	$-$
multiplication	$\times$
division	$\div$
equal to	$=$
not equal to	$\neq$
greater than	$>$
less than	$<$
greater than or equal to	$\geq$
less than or equal to	$\leq$

Time Equivalencies

60 seconds = 1 minute
60 minutes = 1 hour
24 hours = 1 day
7 days = 1 week
12 months = 1 year
52 weeks = 1 year
365 days = 1 year
10 years = 1 decade
100 years = 1 century

Units of Conversion

Length

10 millimeters = 1 centimeter
100 centimeters = 1 meter
1,000 meters = 1 kilometer

Formulas

Area of a Rectangle = length multiplied by width
Area of a Square = length multiplied by width

Cutout 1

Use with page 103.

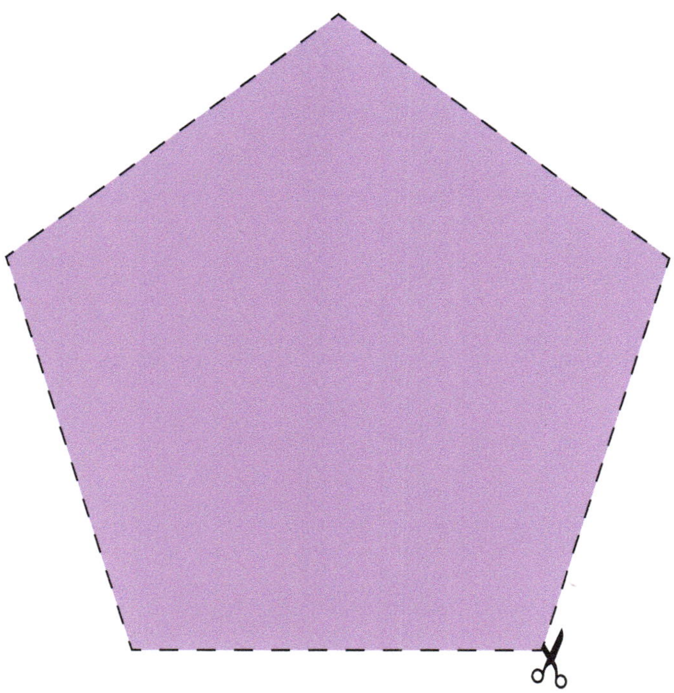

Test 1 Study Page • Review

Remove, answer, and glue in your notebook.

Unit 1: Numbers Up To 100,000

1. Write in word form.

a. 66,583 ▶ ______________________

b. 96,481 ▶ ______________________

c. 35,927 ▶ ______________________

2. Start from the given number and complete the sequence.

a. Forward, by 1,000s.

37,192 , ____ , ____ , ____ , ____ , ____

b. Backward, by 10,000s.

65,439 , ____ , ____ , ____ , ____ , ____

3. Complete the table using the highlighted digit in each number.

	Number	Position	Place Value
a.	49,721		
b.	93,583		
c.	67,401		

4. Match.

a. 36,078 — 3 **Th** + 7 **H** + 9 **T** + 5 **O**

b. 3,795 — 9 **TTh** + 4 **Th** + 6 **H** + 8 **T** + 1 **O**

c. 94,681 — 30,000 + 6,000 + 70 + 8

Name: ______________________________ Grade: __________

Numbers Up To 100,000

Reading Numbers

98,098 is read as
ninety-eight thousand, ninety-eight.

Counting Up To 100,000

By 1,000s ▸ 34,520, 35,520, 36,520
By 10,000s ▸ 18,375, 28,375, 38,375

Place Value

The place value of the digit 7 in
73,000 is 70,000 and in 37,000 it is 7,000.

Composing and Decomposing Numbers

24,318
2 **TTh** + 4 **Th** + 3 **H** + 1 **T** + 8 **O**
20,000 + 4,000 + 300 + 10 + 8

Comparing and Putting Numbers in Order in a Place Value Chart

TTh	Th	H	T	O
6	4	0	0	0

6 **TTh** = 6 **TTh**
4 **Th** < 8 **Th**
64,000 < 68,000

TTh	Th	H	T	O
6	8	0	0	0

Comparing and Putting Numbers in Order on a Number Line

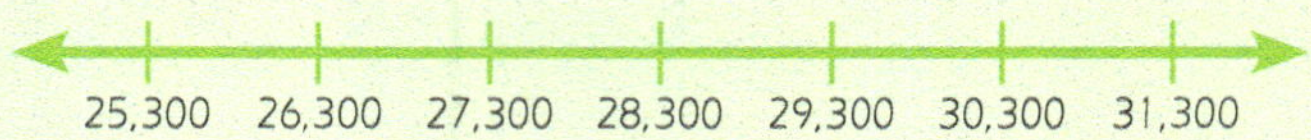

29,000 is to the left of 31,000.
29,300 < 31,300

Test 1 Study Page • Summary

Unit 1: Numbers Up To 100,000

5. Complete the composition or decomposition of the numbers.

a. 74,028 ▶ ___ + ___ + ___ + ___ + ___

b. 96,351 ▶ ___ + ___ + ___ + ___ + ___

c. 50,000 + 6,000 + 900 + 20 + 4 ▶ ___

6. Use the place value chart to put the numbers in order from **least to greatest**.

18,500 , 81,325 , 8,421 , 1,850 , 36,458 , 93,471

HTh	TTh	Th	H	T	O

HTh	TTh	Th	H	T	O

HTh	TTh	Th	H	T	O

HTh	TTh	Th	H	T	O

HTh	TTh	Th	H	T	O

HTh	TTh	Th	H	T	O

______ , ______ , ______ , ______ , ______ , ______

7. Solve.

a. 61,578 + 16,364

c. 97,681 – 35,437

b. 17,623 + 21,158

d. 32,311– 6,534

glue here

glue here

glue here

glue here

glue here

Test 2 Study Page • Summary

Unit 2: Surveys

c. Which is the most popular sport?

____

d. What conclusions can you draw from the chart?

____

2. Read the following situation and do the activities.

Students were asked about their favorite color. These are the results.

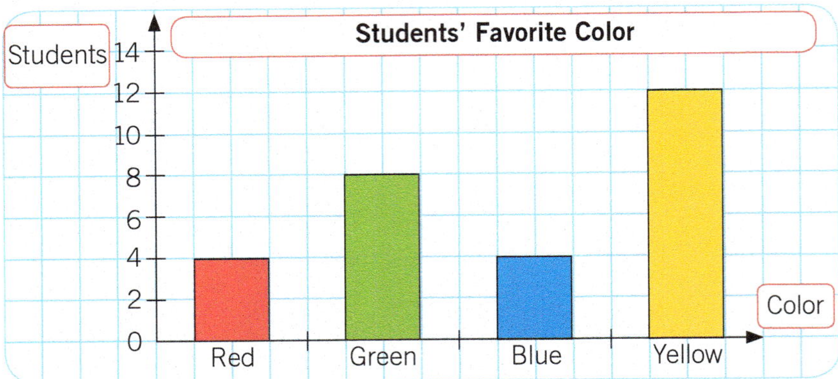

a. Which color is the most popular?

____

b. Which colors are the least popular?

____

c. How many students were surveyed?

Test 3 Study Page • Review

Unit 3: Numbers Up To 1,000,000

Remove, answer, and glue in your notebook

1. Complete with the number or word form.

a. 382,039 ▶ ______________________

b. 729,471 ▶ ______________________

c. 142,989 ▶ ______________________

d. ________ ▶ nine hundred forty thousand, eight hundred thirteen

e. ________ ▶ one hundred fifty thousand, four hundred twenty-three

f. ________ ▶ two hundred ninety thousand, one hundred seventy-eight

2. Complete by composing or decomposing the numbers.

a. ________ ▶ 200,000 + 60,000 + 5,000 + 300 + 70 + 2

b. ________ ▶ 900,000 + 30,000 + 1,000 + 500 + 90 + 8

c. ________ ▶ 7 **HTh** + 4 **TTh** + 9 **Th** + 2 **H** + 1 **T** + 9 **O**

d. ________ ▶ 3 **HTh** + 5 **TTh** + 6 **Th** + 3 **H** + 2 **T** + 4 **O**

e. 836,196 ▶ ______ + ______ + ______ + ______ + ______ + ______

f. 935,121 ▶ ______ + ______ + ______ + ______ + ______ + ______

Name: ____________________ Grade: __________

Numbers Up To 1,000,000

Place Value	The place value of 7 in 730,000 is 700,000 and in 37,000 it is 7,000.
Composing and Decomposing Numbers	700,000 + 20,000 + 9,000 + 400 + 80 + 2 7 **HTh** + 2 **TTh** + 9 **Th** + 4 **H** + 8 **T** + 2 **O** ▶ 729,482 374,193 ▶ 3 **HTh** + 7 **TTh** + 4 **Th** + 1 **H** + 9 **T** + 3 **O** 300,000 + 70,000 + 4,000 + 100 + 90 + 3
Order and Comparison of Numbers	When you compare 871,000 and 895,000: 8 **HTh** = 8 **HTh** 800,000 = 800,000 7 **Th** < 9 **Th** 70,000 < 90,000 871,000 < 895,000 871,000 is less than 895,000.

Test 3 Study Page • Summary

Unit 3: Numbers Up To 1,000,000

3. Mark the number line with intervals, and then put the numbers below in order.

a. 800,000 760,000 820,000 780,000 740,000

b. 120,000 115,000 125,000 110,000 130,000

c. 700,040 400,040 300,040 600,040 500,040

d. 420,000 360,000 330,000 300,000 390,000

e. 260,000 360,000 560,000 160,000 460,000

glue here

glue here

glue here

glue here

glue here

Test 4 Study Page • Review

Unit 4: Fractions and Angles

Remove, answer, and glue in your notebook.

1. Write the fractions in word form.

a. $\frac{3}{7}$ ▶ ______________________________

b. $\frac{7}{10}$ ▶ ______________________________

2. Represent the fraction with a set, on a number line or in a section.

$\frac{3}{5}$

Set

Section

Number Line

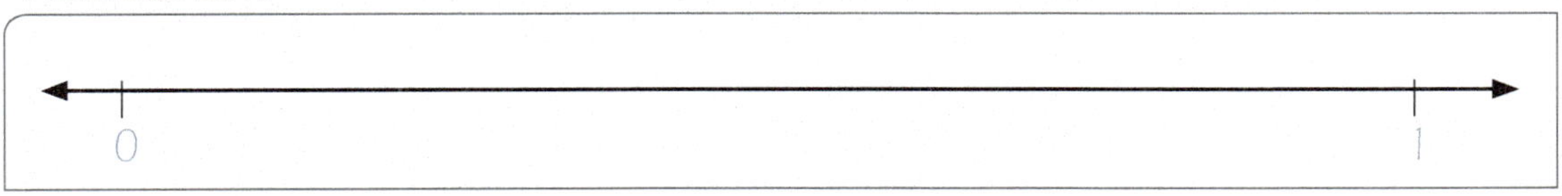

3. Write the mixed number represented.

a.

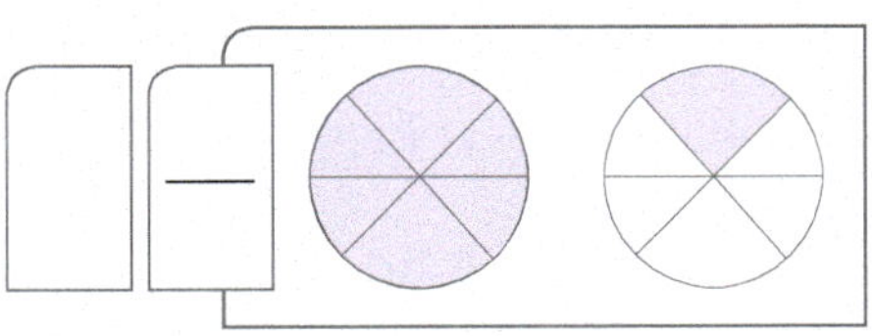

c.

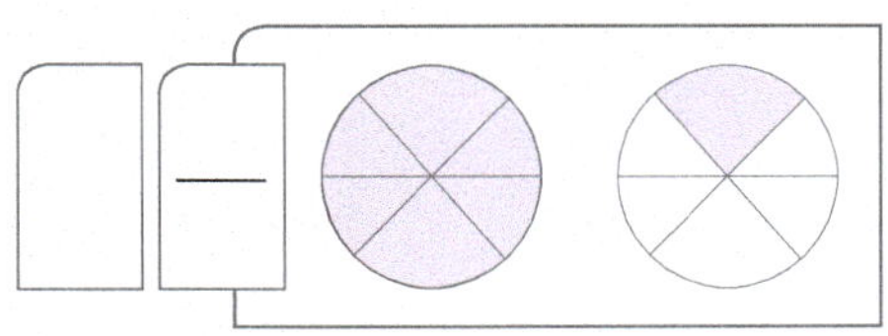

b.

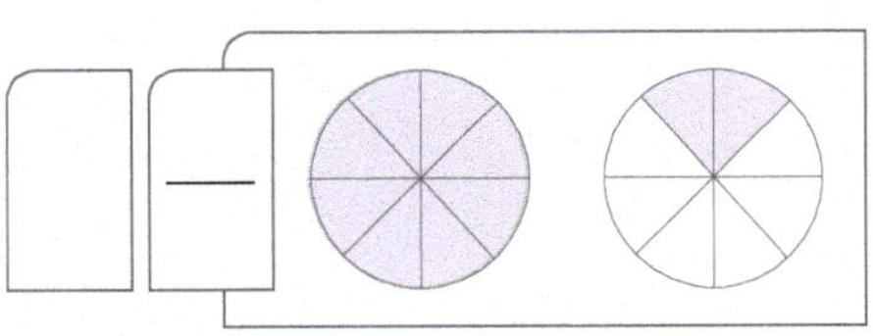

d.

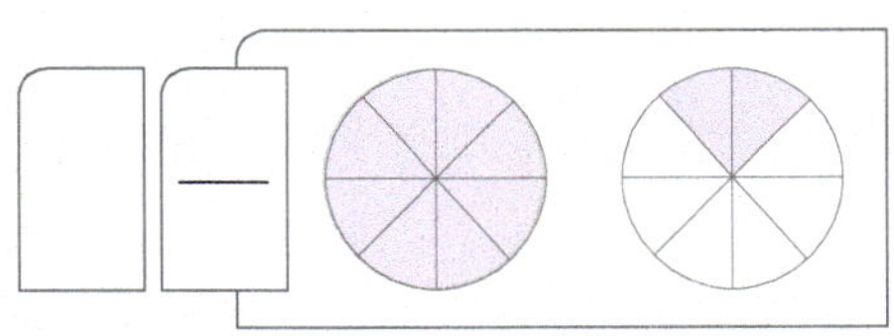

Name: ______________________________ Grade: __________

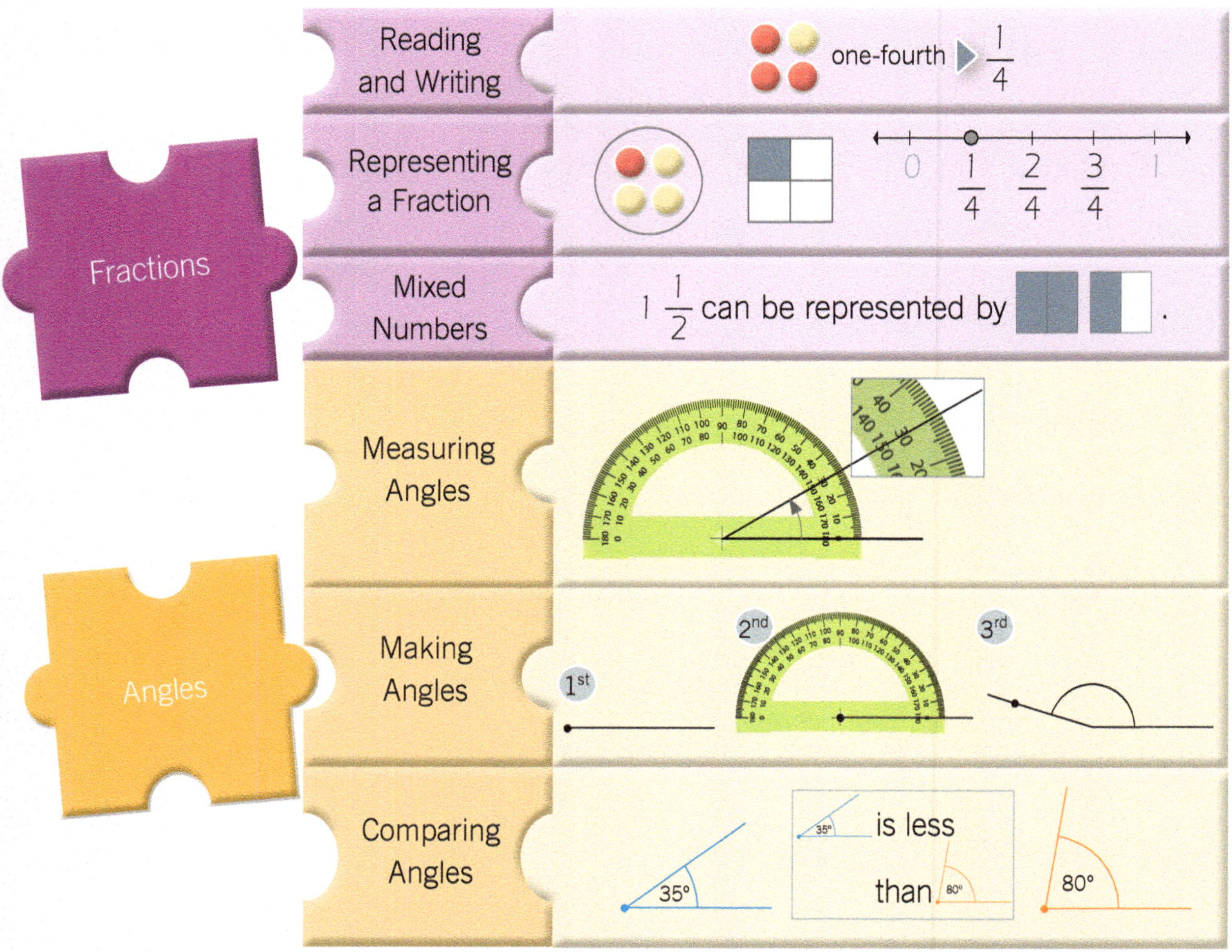

Fractions
Reading and Writing
one-fourth
1/4
Representing a Fraction
0
1/4
2/4
3/4
1
Mixed Numbers
1 1/2 can be represented by
Angles
Measuring Angles
Making Angles
1st
2nd
3rd
Comparing Angles
35°
is less than
80°

Test 4 Study Page • Summary

Unit 4: Fractions and Angles

4. Do the following activities using a protractor.

Measure the angle.

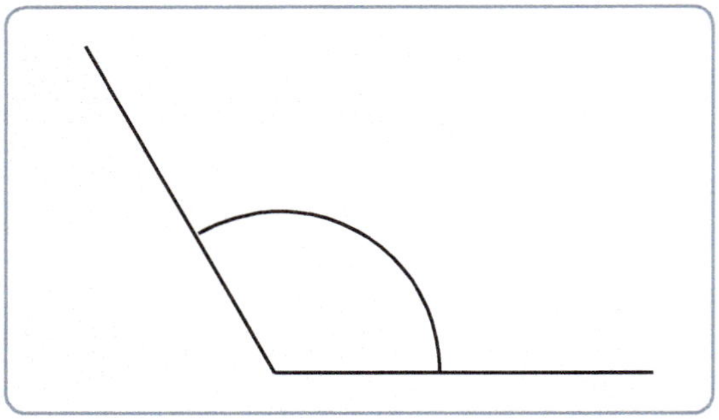

Make a 135° angle.

The angle measures ________.

5. Circle the symmetrical figures and mark the line(s) of symmetry.

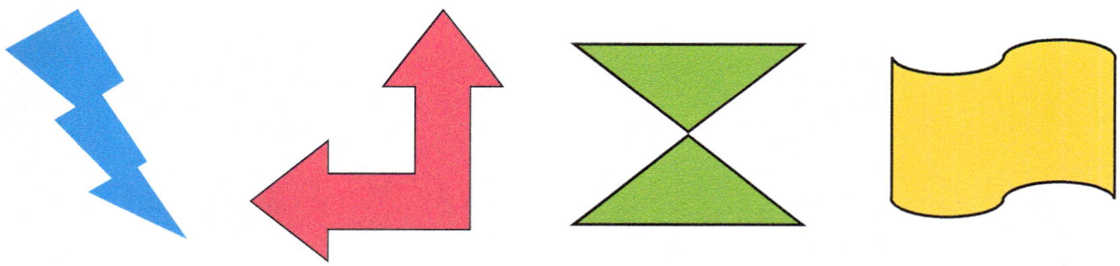

Test 5 Study Page • Review

Unit 5: Measurements

Remove, answer, and glue in your notebook.

1. Write the correct time on each of the clocks.

a. 11 o'clock at night

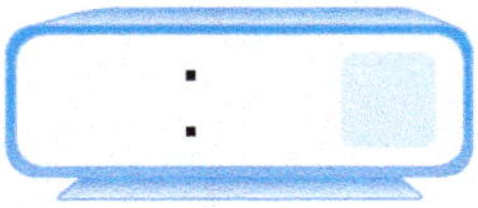

b. seven o'clock in the morning

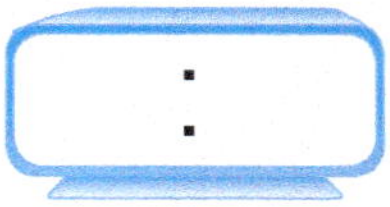

c. six thirty in the evening

2. Complete the equivalences.

a. Two and a half hours ▶ ______ minutes

b. One and a half years ▶ ______ months

c. 3,000 centimeters ▶ ______ meters

d. 7 minutes ▶ ______ seconds

3. Solve the word problem.

Mrs. Sampson has started knitting a scarf for her son. She has finished half a meter, and she wants to knit 90 centimeters more. How long will the scarf be?

Information and its unit of measurement: ➡ ______________________

Strategy used to answer: ➡

Answer in the unit of measurement asked for: ➡ ______________________

Name: ______________________________ Grade: __________

Units of Measurement for Time and Length

Time on Analog and Digital Clocks

Analog Clock

Digital Clock

12-hour format

24-hour format (military time)

Days, Months and Years

1 year = 12 months = 365 days

1 month = 30 days, approximately

Hours, Minutes and Seconds

1 hour = 60 minutes

1 minute = 60 seconds

Meters and Centimeters

1 meter = 100 centimeters

Area and Mass

Area of Squares and Rectangles

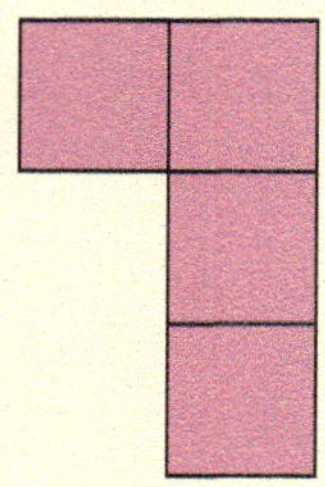

The figure's area is 4 cm^2.

Mass

It is the amount of matter that an object or body has. It is measured using a scale. The units of measurement are grams and kilograms.

Test 5 Study Page • Summary

Unit 5: Measurements

4. Calculate the area of the figures. Each ☐ has an area of 1 cm^2.

a.

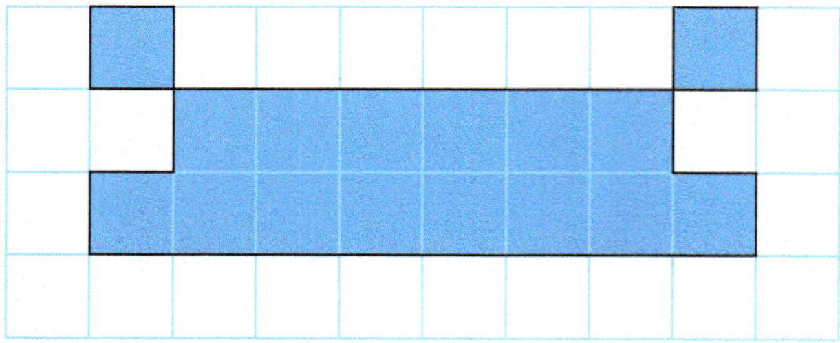

The area is ▶ __________ ☐,

which is equivalent to

__________ cm^2.

b.

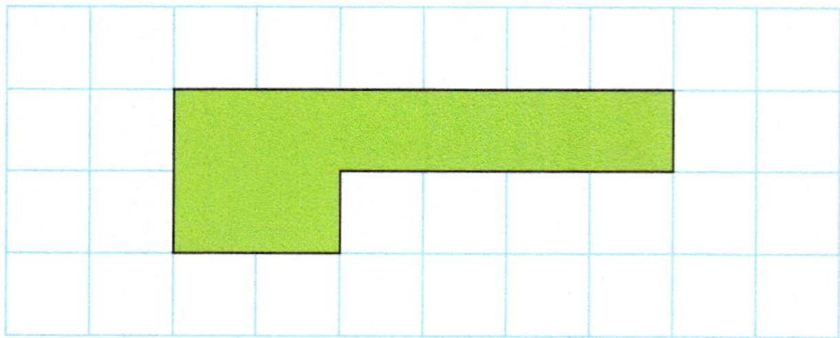

The area is ▶ __________ ☐,

which is equivalent to

__________ cm^2.

5. Complete the expressions of mass with >, < or = .

a. 2,500 g ◯ 1 and a half kg

b. 2 kg ◯ 2,000 g

c. 1,500 g ◯ 15 kg

d. 750 g ◯ $\frac{3}{4}$ kg

Activity Card 1

Use with page 76 of the Student's Book.

Activity Card 2

Use with page 119 of the Student's Book.

2019

January

M	T	W	T	F	S	S
	1	2	3	4	5	6
7	8	9	10	11	12	13
14	15	16	17	18	19	20
21	22	23	24	25	26	27
28	29	30	31			

February

M	T	W	T	F	S	S
				1	2	3
4	5	6	7	8	9	10
11	12	13	14	15	16	17
18	19	20	21	22	23	24
25	26	27	28			

March

M	T	W	T	F	S	S
				1	2	3
4	5	6	7	8	9	10
11	12	13	14	15	16	17
18	19	20	21	22	23	24
25	26	27	28	29	30	31

April

M	T	W	T	F	S	S
1	2	3	4	5	6	7
8	9	10	11	12	13	14
15	16	17	18	19	20	21
22	23	24	25	26	27	28
29	30					

May

M	T	W	T	F	S	S
		1	2	3	4	5
6	7	8	9	10	11	12
13	14	15	16	17	18	19
20	21	22	23	24	25	26
27	28	29	30	31		

June

M	T	W	T	F	S	S
					1	2
3	4	5	6	7	8	9
10	11	12	13	14	15	16
17	18	19	20	21	22	23
24	25	26	27	28	29	30

July

M	T	W	T	F	S	S
1	2	3	4	5	6	7
8	9	10	11	12	13	14
15	16	17	18	19	20	21
22	23	24	25	26	27	28
29	30	31				

August

M	T	W	T	F	S	S
			1	2	3	4
5	6	7	8	9	10	11
12	13	14	15	16	17	18
19	20	21	22	23	24	25
26	27	28	29	30	31	

September

M	T	W	T	F	S	S
						1
2	3	4	5	6	7	8
9	10	11	12	13	14	15
16	17	18	19	20	21	22
23	24	25	26	27	28	29
30						

October

M	T	W	T	F	S	S
	1	2	3	4	5	6
7	8	9	10	11	12	13
14	15	16	17	18	19	20
21	22	23	24	25	26	27
28	29	30	31			

November

M	T	W	T	F	S	S
				1	2	3
4	5	6	7	8	9	10
11	12	13	14	15	16	17
18	19	20	21	22	23	24
25	26	27	28	29	30	

December

M	T	W	T	F	S	S
						1
2	3	4	5	6	7	8
9	10	11	12	13	14	15
16	17	18	19	20	21	22
23	24	25	26	27	28	29
30	31					